PAST LIVES
PRESENT
STORIES

About the Author

Judith Marshall (Salem, MA) has a BA in history, an MA in linguistics, and a lifelong passion for the paranormal. Her personal encounters with the spirit world sparked more than twenty-five years of research into spiritual metaphysics. Visit her online at www.judithmarshallauthor.com.

JUDITH MARSHALL

PAST LIVES PRESENT STORIES

Healing & Wisdom Through
Past Life Exploration

Llewellyn Publications
Woodbury, Minnesota

First Edition
First Printing, 2014

Cover art: iStockphoto.com/27565977/©Leysan
Cover design by Ellen Lawson
Editing by Andrea Neff

Llewellyn Publications is a registered trademark of Llewellyn Worldwide Ltd.

Library of Congress Cataloging-in-Publication Data

Marshall, Judith, 1968–
  Past lives, present stories / by Judith Marshall. — First Edition.
      pages   cm
   ISBN 978-0-7387-3668-6
1. Marshall, Judith, 1968– 2. Reincarnation—Biography. 3.
Reincarnation. I. Title.
   BL520.M37A3 2014
   133.901'35—dc23

                                              2014020477

Llewellyn Publications
A Division of Llewellyn Worldwide Ltd.
2143 Wooddale Drive
Woodbury, MN 55125-2989
www.llewellyn.com

Printed in the United States of America

OTHER BOOKS BY JUDITH MARSHALL

My Conversations with Angels

(Llewellyn Publications, 2012)

CONTENTS

INTRODUCTION

In the summer of 1993, I spent a few hours in Plymouth, England. As I wandered the cobbled, medieval streets of the historic quarter, a sense of déjà vu washed over me. One road in particular stood out, for I seemed to know each twist and turn before it came. After a short time, I came upon the entrance to an Elizabethan garden, and an urge to see it grabbed hold of me.

A sign blocked the entryway: "Closed for maintenance." My heart sank, and I turned to leave.

"Can I help you, Miss?" a deep voice said.

I spun around. A workman in white stood on the threshold. By all appearances, he was a painter, but how he'd materialized so quickly and quietly was a mystery.

"I-I'm only here for a few hours," I stammered, "and I was hoping to see the garden. I see it's closed, though."

"You're American," he said. It wasn't a question.

"I am," I replied.

"And you're alone?" he asked.

"As alone as you can be," I answered.

He looked right and left, then moved the sign. "Come in then, just for a bit."

As I stepped through the archway, I wondered if I'd get him in trouble. On impulse, I turned to thank him.

He was nowhere in sight.

My hands found my hips. "What the—"

Go on, an inner voice advised. *Look around. You're supposed to be here.*

I shrugged, then wandered into the garden. When I reached the heart of the site, I paused. An odd sensation—part premonition, part awe—gripped me. Lightheaded, I looked for a bench.

Flash! It was nighttime. The air was pungent with the warring scents of roses and manure. Beyond the refuge of hedge and herb, horse hooves clopped on stone. Laughter mingled with shouts.

Bam! Daylight returned, and I was back in the present. I took a deep breath and steadied myself. Then I studied my surroundings, acutely aware of what "belonged" and what did not. The Elizabethan stone and hand-carved arches were appropriate; the modern buildings clashed.

Have you or someone you know had a similar experience? Have you ever traveled someplace new and had the creeping suspicion you'd been there before? Have you sensed an immediate connection—positive or negative—with a complete stranger? What about dreams that seem too real to be a kaleidoscope of fantasy, or out-and-out memories that you know stem from another time and place?

Belief in reincarnation is a fundamental element of many philosophical and spiritual traditions, including Hinduism, Buddhism, Jainism, Sikhism, and Taoism. It found a home among the ancient Greeks and Celts and figured in Norse mythology and Inuit traditions. It also appeared in Kabbalistic texts and early Christian writings and persists in Orthodox Judaism and modern Gnosticism.

In the natural world, we need only look to the rhythm of the seasons and the scientific fact that energy is neither created nor destroyed. It simply changes form, not once, but over and over again, ad infinitum.

The list of famous people who've believed in reincarnation runs the gamut: Pythagoras, Socrates, Saint Gregory, Benjamin Franklin, Leo Tolstoy, Mark Twain, Walt Whitman, Ralph Waldo Emerson, Henry Ford, and General George S. Patton, to name only a handful. While those names demand respect, they're not responsible for my beliefs on the subject; experience is the author of that. Sometimes through sight and sound, and always through sensation, intuition, and claircognizance (clear/inner knowing), I was tuned in from the get-go.

Nearly every professional psychic I've encountered has told me I was an author in several lives. That could explain why I penned my first story at age three. Short stories evolved into chapter stories, and soon I was writing elaborate scripts for my dolls to act out. I was in love with language, and there was only one thing I wanted to be when I grew up: a wordsmith.

That desire was ever present, even when I prepared for First Communion in the Catholic Church.

"How can you share God's love with others?" the nuns asked me.

My response was immediate: "By writing stories."

More than three decades later, when I learned I'd been an eighth-century nun who wrote for that very reason, my instinctive response made sense. And it seems I came into the world this time around with a similar purpose in mind.

That intuitive bond with words was always there, and it's one way I receive and decode spiritual guidance, particularly about past-life details. Information flows to me through the way a word sounds or how it looks on the written page. Gut reactions and infusions of knowledge inspire connections I might otherwise have missed.

Vibrant, detailed dreams—many of which have all the earmarks of astral travel—are another way I glean spiritual information. I've learned quite a bit about my past lives through them.

Although I've only uncovered some of those lives, I'm sure more information will unfold at the proper time. But I have to ask the question: was I really those other people or was I just tapping into the energy or consciousness that was once a part of them? Every memory and event has felt incredibly personal, but I don't close the door on other possibilities.

Some of the lives with which I've connected are people recorded in history. My ego balks at the idea that I might've been those individuals. But a calm inner voice whispers: *Fear not. When you and God conceived the plan to serve humanity through the written word, you wanted to make a spiritual impact and fully display the interwoven and limitless splendor of God's love. You were meant to find proof of your other lives, so you needed to become a few prominent people who would leave a trail you could follow.*

I'm not a professional psychic, but I've done the research on reincarnation and had enough personal experience—confirmed by professional psychics, channelers, and others with psychic awareness—to know something about it. Enough so that now, at the age of forty-six, I can share what I've learned and encourage others to look within their own lives for confirmation of the cosmos of immortality and interconnection we're privileged to share.

The information, examples, and exercises in this book will help you do that. You'll deepen your self-knowledge and embrace a larger awareness—and a larger soul—than you ever imagined.

Clues about past lives do lead up to something. Where there's smoke, there's fire. Signs, synchronicities, dreams, memories, and gut reactions to people and places are like a road map leading us home … to all we ever were and all we might yet be.

1

REINCARNATION: EXTREME SPORT FOR THE SOUL

The Other Side, what some might call "heaven," is the utopia for which we yearn in our earthly, everyday lives. Our euphoria knows no bounds. Our spirits are footloose and fancy-free. The love and light of God infuses everyone and everything. (Although I use the word "God" for Universal Intelligence, please feel free to substitute whatever term you prefer.) Yet we choose to leave that state of bliss and lower our vibrations to inhabit the third-dimensional realm of drama and delayed manifestation in restrictive bodies that will experience pain and limitation. Without a doubt, life on the physical plane is the ultimate extreme sport and is not for the faint of heart!

It boggles the mind and begs the question: why do we choose it? Not just once, mind you, but over and over again. What in God's name—and God's image—is the soul up to?

DEFINITION OF THE SOUL

First, let's define what the soul actually is. It is the energy and information of God in miniature. It is pure consciousness, immortal and divine. The human body doesn't contain the soul; the soul contains the body. Your soul is both inside and outside of you at all times, just as God's soul—what Ralph Waldo Emerson called "the Oversoul" and the *Star Wars* saga named "the Force"—contains the universe, flowing in and around everything in existence.

THE PURPOSE OF REINCARNATION

The soul's greatest desire is to know itself experientially. It generates numerous "imperfect" personalities/lifetimes in the physical world so it can know itself as perfect and experience oneness with others and with God.

During a given lifetime, the personality learns lessons, and every experience is imprinted on the soul's memory and stored in the akashic records, which are the sum total of all information—both history and experience—in the universe. Our souls create, co-create, and re-create themselves within each incarnation and across all incarnations.

TIME

Scientists are beginning to understand that the human perception of time, flowing from past to present to future, is an illusion—a grand and convincing one, but an illusion nonetheless. All time exists in "the eternal now," which means that all past, present, and future events are occurring right now. Your soul is actually in and around all of your incarnations at once, and your so-called past and future lives are actually simultaneous lives.

If you've ever felt the emotions and memories of another lifetime bleed into your present, you know this truth on an experiential level. Even in this single lifetime, you are living your past, present, and future all at once. My own children have stopped dead in their tracks to report seeing "past" events from my current life (incidents they didn't see the "first" time around and couldn't possibly know about) "replay" themselves in the exact spot where the events originally occurred. We tend to think of such moments as energy echoes, like residual hauntings in the field of paranormal investigation. But when all time merges into one, a new picture emerges.

Even premonitions are simply picking up on something that's happening right now, our future selves helping us in the present. If it's a personal premonition—one that involves you alone or someone you know—you can change the outcome by altering your "present" actions and creating a new version of your future. Premonitions on a grander scale—those that involve a significant number of people—can also inspire different outcomes, but the larger the party, the greater the challenge.

Since all time is now, you don't have to do anything or believe in one particular creed to gain immortality. You already have it, just by virtue of the fact that you exist. You have to be immortal, because you are here now and all eternity is now.

Of course, in our physical, relative reality, time does exist, and we think in terms of past, present, and future. Enter karma.

KARMA

Karma is a Sanskrit word that means "action" or "deed," and those actions set in motion the universal law of cause and effect (i.e., action and reaction). In other words, you reap what you sow.

Ultimately, our thoughts, words, and deeds stem from either love or fear. Good karma is cultivated by making choices based on love. We emit positive energy, and the universe sends positive energy our way. When fear controls our actions, trouble follows. Holding on to that fear can result in our becoming stuck in a holding pattern of pain and despair. But the law of cause and effect is not a platform for payback or punishment; it's a law of love meant to encourage us to release our fears and choose something better the next time … in this life and in future ones. For instance, a person who abuses children in one life might choose to help children in the next.

If you want to make better choices, listen to your gut. Your body's innate intelligence is linked to your intuition, which has a direct line of communication with your soul. Because your soul knows your past, present, and potential future, it'll steer you in the right direction. If your intestines—or your instincts—find a particular thought indigestible, let it go and think a new, more positive thought. If something you've said or done makes you sick to your stomach or gives you a heavy heart, acknowledge it, forgive yourself, and resolve to do better next time. In this way, you'll create better "effects" for your present and future self.

Prior to birth, we make spiritual contracts with others we've known in previous lives. Often, these contracts produce a form of "payment in kind." For example, a chiropractor who's helped me to heal in this life is someone I healed in a previous one.

Karmic payment can also come in the form of a windfall. At such moments, positive, loving energy—built up for days, weeks, even centuries—targets a single point of focus and creates a miracle.

I experienced such a windfall when I was twenty-eight. Six months before it occurred, I developed pleural bruising of the chest wall, which turned breathing into an exercise in torture. Even after I recovered, I wasn't up to par. Trifling colds became bronchitis overnight.

Months later, my parents and I traveled together to Wales, and I caught a cold on the flight over. Within two days of our arrival, my voice dropped nearly an octave and my chest burned with the slightest cough. My father had also hurt his right knee just before the trip, and after two days of climbing castle stairs, he was in pain. Clearly, our vacation had begun on a poor note.

The night we settled into our Pembrokeshire bed and breakfast, my father and I fell into a deep sleep. My mother, however, did not. She fretted about my health and feared my lungs would never recover from the effects of the pleural bruising. All night, she lay awake praying for my healing and, ultimately, my life.

Unaware of her long vigil, I woke the following morning to an image—a mere flash—of her as a nun in another life, kneeling on a cold stone floor with hands folded in prayer. Perplexed, I brushed the vision aside and hacked all the way to the bathroom.

Even as we set out for St. David's Cathedral, my dad and I remained ignorant of my mom's fervent prayers. But I was quite aware that we were approaching a sacred site of pilgrimage and miraculous healings—for both pagans and Christians—and a purported intersection of ley lines.

Once inside the cathedral, my father went off to explore on his own. My mother and I remained in the nave, but I veered a few yards away from her and gazed up at what seemed a massive time machine to the High Middle Ages. The Transitional Norman architecture was a masterwork of carving, with its great rounded arches and intricate wooden ceiling.

All at once, heat poured through me, and my flesh began to tingle. The next instant, I felt as if something was pulling me downward, literally rooting me to the spot where I stood. I remained upright but seemed paralyzed by the bizarre suction.

My mother hastened toward me. "Jude, are you all right? You look faint."

I wasn't sure, but suddenly I could move my feet. I found the nearest pew and dropped onto it. Little by little, normality returned, but I couldn't shake the feeling that something powerful had occurred.

When we met up with my dad, he mentioned feeling an odd sensation of heat in his right knee. Then I knew: he and I had received healings. By that evening, we felt remarkably better. The next morning, I was completely well, and my lungs have functioned beautifully ever since. I believe the "miracle" resulted from a combination of my mother's prayers and a long-postponed karmic payment from a Welsh lifetime in which my parents and I helped others and had total faith in that location's power.

RESULTS OF EXPLORATION

Your reasons for exploring other lifetimes will be personal and, most likely, private. Even with simple curiosity as your motive, you have everything to gain. Two of the most tangible benefits are healing and understanding. Let's look at each in turn.

Healing

You may or may not have physical signs of trauma from a previous life, but there have been many documented cases of such. Inexplicable pain, chronic conditions, deformities, and even birthmarks can be linked to harrowing events—anything from torture to fatal wounds—from another life.

Dr. Ian Stevenson (1918–2007), a psychiatrist and director of the Division of Perceptual Studies at the University of Virginia School of Medicine, became known internationally for his reincarnation research. His work with children who remembered past lives produced remarkable evidence. Some of the children who reported a violent, past-life death had birthmarks that corresponded directly to the location of their past fatal wounds. One child who recalled dying from a gunshot wound to the head had birthmarks that matched the entrance and exit wounds he sustained in his previous life. Present deformities and missing appendages also corresponded to past-life injuries some had suffered.

Unearthing specific instances in past lives is often a tool for healing. The famous healer and psychic Edgar Cayce (March 18, 1877–January 3, 1945) gave more than 14,000 readings, and 1,920 of them were "life readings" that found past-life issues affecting clients' physical, mental, and emotional condition in the present. Today, Dr. Brian Weiss and Dr. Bruce Goldberg are at the forefront of past-life research and regression therapy.

In my own life, I've had a sixteen-year love-hate relationship with my lower back, and I believe this struggle is connected to a past life. The trouble—in this life—began one afternoon just after my thirtieth birthday. I sat cross-legged on my bedroom floor, hunched over my laptop computer, lost in my writing. I had no idea eight hours had passed until I tried to stand.

Pain seized my lower back with an intensity I could never have imagined. Bending over for such an extended period, I later learned, is one of the worst things you can do to your back. My eight-hour stint—or stunt, you might say—conferred upon me two bulging disks and a mass of scar tissue.

Time is indeed relative, because the next couple of months dragged on at a snail's pace. My back got worse, and since disks were involved, sitting was torture. It healed partially, but a few years later, it contributed to a hellish period of chronic pelvic pain. At its worst, the pain was a phantom knife that jabbed and twisted my left ovary, uterus, bladder, and urethra; the rest of the time it was a constant, merciless pin pricking those same areas. Despite a number of specialists, a torrent of tests, and exploratory surgery, I remained a medical mystery for ten excruciating months.

Looking back, I realize both events were clues to a past life in seventeenth-century England during which I was accused of witchcraft and tortured by the self-proclaimed "Witch-finder General," Matthew Hopkins. If no "devil's mark" was found on the accused witches' bodies, he often forced them to sit cross-legged on a table or stool, in which position they were bound and left for up to twenty-four hours. And when he and his cronies searched the bodies of suspected witches for devil's marks, they used a needle or blade to prick them, with particular attention paid to the genitalia. It seems my body relived incidents from a previous life so that past pain could rise to the surface and be healed.

Some people work with past-life regressionists to heal physical conditions, but I didn't go that route. Once I found the right chiropractic care, everything changed. Today, the pelvic pain is old history, and although my lower back is still a challenge, it's much better than it used to be.

Discovering the root cause of emotional pain, fears, pho-bias, and thorny relationships can go a long way toward heal-ing them. Imagine learning that someone who wronged you in this life is actually someone you wronged in a previous life. It could pave the way for smoother relations between the two of you and expedite forgiveness. And the act of forgiveness—of another or one's self—truly heals.

Understanding

Similar themes and archetypes pop up in different lifetimes: the same lessons, the same type of life, etc. Uncovering these forgotten connections can help you understand your current self better: your desires, your fears, your career, your relationships, etc. For instance, I've always had a thing about being falsely accused. The few times it happened, it stung me to the core and I overreacted. I also avoid courtroom dramas—whether on TV or the silver screen—like the plague. If unable to defend myself against a false accusation, I freak. All of that stems from past-life accusations of *maleficia* ("evil doings") and from a life in which I was accused of being a traitor and then denied the chance to plead my case.

Past lives fuel not only our current emotions but also our fascination with certain people and places. In addition, they inspire a number of paranormal experiences, although you might not be aware of the significance until hindsight kicks in. Learning specifics about those lives can help you connect the dots.

I grew up in Florida, but when I was seven, my paternal grandparents took me and my older brother to visit relatives in Ohio. After sundown, their crisp, cool backyard was a veritable fairyland. My brother and I marveled at the myriad lightning bugs dancing and darting from this branch to that. We were so enchanted, we caught a few and placed them in a glass jar.

Our innocent goal was to prolong our sense of wonder. The only trouble was I forgot to punch holes in the cap. When the inevitable occurred, my brother accepted the fireflies' deaths with flawless composure and went on with his evening unaffected. I, on the other hand, lost it.

I was inconsolable, crying tears of guilt and compassion for hours. My mind—and my harried grandparents—told me they were just insects. My heart screamed that all of life was connected, and in my neglect, I'd murdered some of nature's perfect creations. My grandfather had no patience for such a sensitive child and made fun of my reaction, which only added fuel to the emotional fire blazing within me.

All living things had value, even a firefly!

That same friction between head and heart resurfaced two decades later the first time (in this life) I learned of the symbols, guides, and spirit helpers known as animal totems. My logical mind questioned the concept, but my heart heard echoes from an incarnation in which all life forms were revered, and accepted it at once. Right away, I knew that two of my animal totems were the wolf and the spider. Both had visited me since childhood in dreams and the waking world.

At the time, I was an airline employee, and I used my flight privileges to attend Native American powwows in New Mexico, Minnesota, Montana, and South Dakota. With my blond hair and pale skin, I stood out like the sorest thumb imaginable, but I didn't care. I loved the drumming, the dancing, and the people. I resonated with their spiritual traditions and experienced a symphony of synchronicity on each trip.

Back home, I shared my exploits with my friend Sylvia, who is a professional psychic. She listened with the same quiet composure with which she greeted everything. Then one day, she gave it to me straight.

"You were a medicine woman in another life," she said. "A healer."

"How do you know?" I asked.

She gave me a pointed look. "That's my job."

That was just the beginning of revelations about a Native American past life. All paved the way for greater understanding.

Exploring and contemplating other lifetimes reminds us that life moves in cycles, in natural rhythms, with a balance of masculine and feminine energies—the yin and the yang—existing in all. We each have male and female aspects within us in our current lifetime, and we've been both genders in other lifetimes.

We've all been rich and poor, saints and "sinners," and every archetype in existence. No guilt trips—or ego trips—required! It's all a part of the balance, a part of our souls experiencing all there is to experience.

2

YOUR PSYCHIC SENSES

Now is a good time to discuss the mechanics of how you'll receive much of the past-life information that comes your way. You'll detect valuable clues by tuning in to the psychic ability you already possess. And yes, everyone has psychic ability, whether they recognize it or not. First off, let's try an experiment.

Give yourself two to three minutes to complete this exercise, and do it somewhere quiet. Now, close your eyes and imagine you're relaxing at the beach. After a few minutes, open your eyes and consider your experience.

What do you remember most? The picture you created in your mind? Vivid colors? If so, clairvoyance might be your primary source of information. Maybe you heard seagulls overhead, children laughing, or waves crashing on the shore.

If so, clairaudience might be your thing. If you felt the sun's heat on your skin, wind blowing your hair, or grains of sand slipping through your fingers or toes, you're probably inclined toward clairsentience. Perhaps you had an instant understanding of why you were there, who you were with, and an entire backstory to go along with it, in which case you could be claircognizant. If you actually smelled the salty air (clairalience) or tasted the drink you imagined sipping (clairgustance), there's a good chance that you're not only predisposed to clairsentience but also have a highly developed sense of intuition.

Most people have a primary and secondary means of receiving psychic information, but if you stay open and alert, the other channels will wend their way into your experience. Clairvoyance, clairaudience, clairsentience, claircognizance, and intuition are invaluable to past-life discovery. Let's look at each in turn.

CLAIRVOYANCE (CLEAR SEEING)

Clairvoyance is the ability to see things that are not visible to the naked eye or that come from another dimension: auras, chakras (energy centers of the human body), occurrences or health-related issues inside the body, objects or events from the past, future events, and ghosts, angels, or other inhabitants of the spirit world. You see them through dreams, physical eyesight, and visions—either static images or a running "movie"—in the mind's eye.

Here's an example of clairvoyance in a dream. I was nineteen at the time and had traveled that day from Dublin to

Cork. Ireland was also the setting for my dream, and I had the sense of a harbor and men speaking in another language about rigging a ship. I also knew that I (a past-life "I") couldn't travel home but had to venture abroad. Suddenly, a Norse longship appeared before me. Seconds later, it morphed into a Norse-Gaelic vessel I later learned was a birlinn, a variant of the longship that was especially used in the Hebrides and West Highlands of Scotland and that still survives as a heraldic symbol (the lymphad, from Gaelic *longfhada*, meaning "longship"). Finally, I saw a coin—with a cross at its center—that was apparently so significant, it zoomed right up to my face and claimed my entire field of vision.

Years later, I researched coins of the period and matched the dream image with a Hiberno-Norse penny minted in Dublin at the end of the tenth century. The coin was rare but very real, and my clairvoyant vision sprang from a past-life memory so strong, it pummeled through the peace of sleep and demanded to be heard. In that life, I was a Hebridean woman who traveled from Dublin to Iceland on a boat like the one in my dream.

If you have a tendency toward clairvoyance in dreams, chances are you'll experience it in the waking world from time to time. It can appear as one or more images that flash before you or a movie that plays in your mind's eye.

One afternoon when my children—Connor and Geoffrey—were three, they sat watching an episode of *Jonny Quest*. A black panther slunk onto the screen, and since the boys had never seen such a huge cat, I wondered what they'd make of it.

All of a sudden, a faraway look washed over Geoffrey's face. "*Me-a-r-h*," he pronounced, slowly, carefully, as though tasting a fine wine. "*Mearh.*"

Anglo-Saxon, I thought, not sure why I thought it.

I went to the closest bookcase and grabbed *A Guide to Old English*, which I'd bought on a whim twelve years earlier from a used bookshop in Galway, the very evening I returned from a trip to the Benedictine convent Kylemore Abbey.

According to the glossary, *mearh* meant "horse."

Unbidden, a vision flashed before my eyes of an Anglo-Saxon man on a black horse thundering across the English countryside at night on an urgent mission.

That's Geoffrey, I thought. Then the image vanished.

On impulse, I phoned a friend, Bożena, and told her about Geoffrey's strange utterance and the vision it inspired.

"You should write about this," she said. "The moment you mentioned looking up the Old English word, I got the same picture in my head that you did."

"What?" I said. "The man on the horse? The English countryside at night?"

"All of it," she confirmed.

It was one of many puzzle pieces that fell into place with a past life in which I wrote about supernatural events and my friend and I were Anglo-Saxon Benedictine nuns. Geoffrey also seems to have played a role in that lifetime.

Trust me. If you and another person share a clairvoyant vision, you're on to something!

CLAIRAUDIENCE (CLEAR HEARING)

Clairaudience is the ability to hear music, voices, or other sounds that originate in another dimension. When you hear a voice, it can sound like your own voice or someone else's.

Dreams are the perfect venue for clairaudience. Angels and spirit guides take particular advantage of them. Your soul, via one of your past-life selves, might also speak to you. So if you're ever in a dream and hear a disembodied voice, pay attention to it!

When I first moved into my husband Dan's apartment, my dreams became more vivid and packed with information. In one of them, I stood before a tall, thin castle flanked by woodland and canopied by a gray sky. Someone close to me—a male family member—had been captured, and I'd just received word that he would be taken far to the north and west of where he'd originally been held. I started toward the castle and was only half conscious of lifting my long skirt so I could climb the stairs without tripping. My mind was abuzz with worry and whispers.

A ransom. A boat. They're going to Beaumaris.

The castle was dark inside, but it matched my mood. I leaned against a long, wooden table and hung my head.

Beaumaris, a disembodied voice urged me. *You must remember Beaumaris.*

I woke with a start. Beaumaris? What the heck was that? A surname? A place?

First thing the following morning, I looked it up. Beaumaris was the name of a town and castle on the Isle of Anglesey in Wales. Years later, I learned about a life in fifteenth-century Ireland in which Dan was again my husband. He was captured by the English and imprisoned first in London and then on the Isle of Man. Beaumaris was a logical stopping and/or launching point on the journey to Man.

Of course, clairaudience also occurs during waking hours, a fact with which Dan and our children are familiar. One morning when the boys were six, I told Dan about a dream I'd had the night before. I rode through the night sky on a large creature I couldn't see but whose back felt as soft as silk. I knew with every fiber of my being that it was an alternate form of one of my spirit guides.

"I keep hearing the word 'kestrel,'" Dan said. It was definitely a message from Spirit.

It wasn't blatant enough, apparently, because some time later, Geoffrey approached me while I sat at the computer. "The giant owls are right there looking at you," he said, pointing to a spot not three yards away.

From the time the boys could speak, they spoke of two "giant owls," which could appear anywhere. Once, Connor described them as tall men with big wings and glowing eyes (angels?), but otherwise, they were giant owls, and they always came as two.

"I heard them too," Geoffrey said. "It was like a whoosh, and then they said 'hawk.'"

My memory stirred. I'd heard the name "Black Hawk" in meditation years before, and with no knowledge of that fact, three different psychics over the previous four years had mentioned that same name to me. They said he was one of my guides and I was some kind of healer. Why I didn't check before, I'll never know, but now I had to learn whether a "Black Hawk" existed in recorded history.

Late eighteenth, early nineteenth centuries, I thought as I turned back to the computer.

Then I caught myself in the act. Had the information come from my subconscious or from the "giant owls"? I shrugged and typed the name into a search engine.

Sure enough, a Sauk warrior named Black Hawk had lived from 1767 to 1838. His full name was Black Sparrow Hawk, and the sparrow hawk was known as the American kestrel.

Kestrel … the same word Dan had heard! I soon learned more about that guide, and in so doing, I discovered more about a previous life in which we were related.

CLAIRSENTIENCE (CLEAR FEELING)

Clairsentience is the ability to experience thoughts, messages, emotions, or physical feelings—especially someone else's, including "another you" from a different life—as an emotional or bodily sensation. It includes gut feelings and physical sensations such as changes in temperature or air pressure, tingling, and goose bumps, even in hot temperatures.

Dan and I honeymooned in Ireland, and my reasons for planning the trip were twofold: (1) Dan had always wanted to go there, and (2) I had a gut feeling that we were supposed to travel there together. After a three-night stay in a tower room at Dromoland Castle, we spent the bulk of our honeymoon at the Lake Hotel in Killarney. I didn't know it at the time, but both locations were connected to my past lives.

The day before our flight home, we traveled back to County Clare and went to Bunratty Castle. The great vaulted hall of the Main Guard is one of the first sights upon entering the castle, but for some reason we saved it for last. After we'd oohed and aahed over the room's treasures, a small gate at one corner caught our attention. We passed through it and descended the stairs to the dungeon.

As one, we peered down into the deep hole. About a minute later, Dan felt claustrophobic. He didn't want to think about the prisoners who'd languished in that pit, so he left the dungeon.

Why I stayed, I don't know. There was no one blocking my exit. In fact, there was no one else inside, but I felt rooted to the spot. Although my feet seemed heavy, the rest of me became light. Nausea seized me, only to be replaced seconds later by dizziness.

I had to get out of there!

I spun around and started up the steps, only half conscious of my feet connecting with them. The stone above the doorway was so low, I conked my forehead on the way out, but I barely felt it. Stunned, I emerged into the hall, into freedom.

Dan rushed to my side. He said I looked pale and shaky and helped me sit down.

All at once, the weight of the world crashed down on me. Desperation. Torment. Grief.

I gasped for air and slapped a hand to my chest, where my heart felt heavy and full. That sensation worked its way up my throat and escaped as a sob.

The emotion held me for scarcely a minute, but that was one minute too long. There was nothing to do but cry it out.

Once I did, I felt completely well. I wiped the tears from my cheeks and grabbed a tissue from my pocket. Without ritual or reserve, I blew my nose.

What I felt wasn't sympathy for past captives, nor was it melodramatics. At the time, I figured I'd been a human sponge for the energy of anguish that still lingered in the space. Maybe I'd connected with a psychic imprint or a long-lost soul. It would be years before I realized that soul was either Dan's or my own.

We were so in tune—even then—that we often read each other's thoughts and absorbed each other's energy. Maybe I "soaked up" his torment from a past-life imprisonment, or perhaps I touched a long-buried nerve of my own from that lifetime. It didn't matter; at our core, we were one and the same.

Clairsentience also includes actual touches from invisible guests. During the ten-month physical hell I described in chapter 1, the memory of my spontaneous healing at St. David's Cathedral began to dominate my thoughts, and I wondered if such a miracle might occur again. Signs and synchronicity seemed to support a trip to Wales, so Dan and I scraped our money together and booked a one-week visit.

The flight there was difficult. Sitting was excruciating; standing was exhausting. Except for our takeoff and landing, I alternated between kneeling and pacing the aisles. By the time we arrived, my spine felt like it would snap in two, and the nonstop pain jumped back and forth between the front of my pelvis and my lower back. But I glimpsed a light at the end of the tunnel, for we would soon reach St. David's.

Two days later, we entered the cathedral, and I went off on my own. I intended to move slowly through each section and let the energy seep into my bones. I spent a good deal of time in the nave and then proceeded to the various chapels.

Although I sensed a shift in energy, it wasn't as intense as on my first visit. I heaved a massive sigh.

Defeated, I stepped into the solitude of the choir. That's when everything changed. The stalls seemed to waver in front of me. I blinked, and all was still. Frowning, I crouched to study the medieval floor tiles.

Lie down, an inner voice urged. *Get down on the floor and be still.*

But there was a lot more to investigate. I stood and glanced at a coat of arms painted on one of the benches. My entire spine seemed ready to give out, but how could I lie down? This was a public place, and a sacred one at that. Besides, I had to keep moving, seeking, praying, and pleading. There must be more I could do to catalyze a healing.

No. Stop where you are and lie down.

I gave in and stretched my back along the hard, cool tiles. All at once, a rush of energy surrounded me and pinned me to the ground. I couldn't budge.

It was neither exhaustion nor imagination. Something held me down.

If it was an angel, it was huge. But it felt like more than one presence. My arms and legs were held fast; so too were my torso and shoulders. Something resembling a hand vibrated against my forehead.

It appeared that my angels and guides had gotten fed up with my antics and joined forces for an intervention. I could almost hear their words.

Enough, Judy. Your healing is nowhere outside of you. You called forth this experience, so absorb the energy, take it with you, and connect with the one who understands this truth: the power that flows through this place is the same that flows within you. It is yours to command.

With difficulty, I rolled onto my side and pushed myself into a sitting position. Then I stood and returned to the nave. That's when I noticed an elderly couple seated nearby. The woman made eye contact with me, then quickly averted her gaze. Worried I'd somehow offended her, I moved away, but thanks to the acoustics, I heard every hushed word she said to her companion.

"Did you see that girl?" she asked. "She's been walking round this place all alone, all the time staring up like she's talking to the saints, like she sees something high in the rafters. I can't explain it, but she looks like a nun of old... holy... like she belongs here. I tell you, it's creepy."

Obviously, I'd made an impression and not necessarily a good one. Feeling a little like a freak, I searched for Dan. It was time to leave.

That night in our bed and breakfast, searing pain ripped through my pelvis. Dan stayed awake as long as he could, but he eventually crashed. Sleep for me was out of the question, so I just lay in bed, staring at the low ceiling. You'd think I would've cried, but I was either too dehydrated or too numbed by the day's events to do so.

In an attempt to achieve a miracle of mind over matter, I controlled my breathing and envisioned white light flooding my pelvis. I held the image for quite a while, but that angry portion of my body refused to be appeased.

If anyone is with me right now, please help me to relax, I thought.

Immediately, the same energetic hand I'd felt in the cathedral pressed against my forehead. The tingling sensation was soothing, as was the thought that I wasn't alone, but sleep was still impossible. The night stretched longer than I ever could've imagined. Each time the pain intensified, I asked for help. And each time, the loving hand obliged me.

As dawn approached, I turned once again to prayer. *God, I can't do this anymore. Help me fall asleep. But don't let me wake up if the pain is still there. Take me in my sleep and let it all be over. Dan will be okay without me. So will my family.*

Once more, the energetic hand covered my forehead.

But if you really want me to stay, I continued, *I'll try. Just lead me to my purpose and help me fulfill it.*

After a few more days, we traveled home, and I eventually found the help I needed. But even as I healed, I contemplated the spiritual aid I'd received in Wales. Angels were present, to be sure, but so was a spirit guide named Gwendolyn, whom I'd known in a past life in Wales. The energetic hand that repeatedly touched my forehead was hers.

If you lean toward clairsentience, there's one other phenomenon you might experience. When you speak a foreign language you knew in a previous life—or pronounce sounds from that language that either don't exist in English or aren't common within a single English word—you might feel a little thrill or a sense of recognition. It may seem crazy, but the language feels good on your tongue.

For as long as I can remember, the short "a" (as in the word "hat") and the fricative "th" (whether voiced as in "this" or voiceless as in "thin") were my favorite sounds of speech. In Old English, those sounds are represented by the ash, eth, and thorn symbols (Æ, æ/Ð, ð/Þ, þ, respectively). Love at first sight was my reaction the first time I saw those letters in a book. And the first time I heard Old English? Don't even get me started!

I reveled in those sounds and loved pronouncing them. I didn't understand why, but I knew they were important somehow. Even as a little girl, I enjoyed speaking the name of an older relative, Aunt Ethel. Her job as an English professor and travels to the British Isles fascinated me, and I intuitively connected her name with the history of the English language and England itself.

During past-life research as an adult, a rush of excitement lit up my soul when I finally linked all of that history to one name: Aethelthryth (Æðelþryð). She was a Benedictine abbess in seventh-century England and was one of my past-life identities.

Claircognizance (Clear Knowing)

Claircognizance is the ability to receive information, ideas, or an overwhelming, all-encompassing sense of knowing out of the blue, often downloaded from the akashic records. Claircognizants simply *know*, even if they're not sure how they know. Although it can happen for no apparent reason, it can also be triggered by touch, sound, or sight. Other times, it immediately follows the comprehension of new data; in other words, knowledge feeds knowledge. Here are some examples.

When I was twenty-five and living in Salem, Massachusetts, my friend Sylvia introduced me to her little brother, José, who was visiting from Costa Rica.

To say that José and I felt an attraction is to say Steven Spielberg is a guy who likes movies. His Latin lover looks and my "mating call dress" were only part of the equation. Yes, there was sexual attraction, but it bowed to an instant recognition of souls.

We weren't the only ones who noticed the connection. The day we met, we attended an event at Sylvia's New Age store, and more than one psychic regarded us with a gleam in the eyes and a grin on the lips. One even winked at me. Another got me alone to describe the "beautiful interaction" she observed between José's aura and mine.

That night, José and I chilled at his sister's condominium. We sat side by side on a cushiony couch, and he reached for my hand. As our flesh melded, I received impressions of our possible past. We'd been lovers more than once; I'd rejected him, and he'd rejected me. We'd been friends, and we'd been family. At least one trip to Earth had a Spanish link that had nothing to do with Costa Rica.

Physical contact—our holding hands—seemed to be the catalyst. Years later, I learned specifics about three lifetimes in which we were not only acquainted, but close.

When my son Connor started babbling as a baby, sound sparked a moment of claircognizance in me. Often, he ended a string of connected sounds with a glottal stop (when the epiglottis stops the flow of air in the throat). All languages make use of glottal stops, but where Connor placed them was characteristic of Japanese speech, in which the sound is used as a verbal period or exclamation mark.

The first time he did it, I thought it was interesting. The fifth time, I thought something else.

He lived in Japan in another life. He was a warrior.

A few years later, I consulted a well-known psychic duo with a great track record. They channeled Spirit through automatic writing and confirmed much of what I already knew or suspected about my past lives and my family's. With no knowledge of Connor's speech patterns or the information I had received through claircognizance, they told me Connor had lived a past life in Japan as a samurai.

Claircognizance via a visual trigger occurred during my sophomore year at Florida State University (FSU). While studying in the library for a history exam, I spied a photo of a letter written by Henry VIII. I looked hard at it, and something stirred in the pit of my stomach.

I know that handwriting, I thought. *I've seen it before.*

I racked my brain to remember where and when I'd seen it. A PBS documentary? No. During a trip to England? Absolutely not.

The sense of recognition was so strong, I couldn't write it off as coincidence. I assumed the answer was locked in my subconscious, and it would be two decades before I learned that Henry was still King of England when last I saw his handwriting.

Historical research offers a potential jackpot if you lean toward claircognizance. As you read facts, you might experience a download of related information on the spot. You might know instantly whether a historian's theory is true or false. And as incredible as it may seem, you could read a person's name "for the first time" and simply *know* that you knew him or her in another life.

INTUITION

Intuition is strongly linked to three of the known "clairs." Sometimes you get a gut feeling, which is clairsentience at play. Other times it informs your mind and resembles clair-cognizance. However, with intuition, you suspect something; with claircognizance, you know without a doubt. Intuition can also result from clairaudience, in which case you've heard an angel or other spirit's message without realizing it.

But intuition goes beyond those senses. It stems from that core part inside you that is one with God/Universal Intelligence. Its perspective is cosmic and contextual. When you listen to intuition, you're connecting with your soul.

Intuition can feel like something you've always known. It can also function as a psychic "alarm clock" that jolts your awareness and facilitates moments of spiritual discovery.

When I was in fifth grade, our class worked together to produce a "newspaper" of historical events, reported as if they were current. While exploring potential topics, one stood out to my ten-year-old mind: the Salem witch trials.

"I have to go there someday," I told a classmate.

"Why?" she asked.

I shrugged. "I don't know, but I'm gonna."

This early impulse was overshadowed by so many others, I almost forgot about it. But when I was twenty-five, it clamored for the spotlight. I was roasting under Florida's relentless sun in my family's backyard when inspiration struck.

I sprinted into the house and called information to obtain the phone number for the Salem Chamber of Commerce.

Within an hour, I'd made a number of calls, and the plan was set in motion.

By late afternoon, when my mother suggested we go to a local theater to see *Hocus Pocus* (filmed on location in Salem), I realized the move was a done deal. Throughout the movie, I honed in on the background, all but ignoring the plot. I saw myself living there. There was nothing to do but trust intuition and pack my bags.

The instant I hit Salem, I knew I was home. "The Witch City" seemed to agree, because everything fell into place. A real estate agent showed me only one apartment, which was perfect for my needs. It was a block away from my bed and breakfast and within two blocks of most of the *Hocus Pocus* locations.

Next came my job search. I pounded the pavement of Derby and Essex Streets, handing my résumé to anyone who'd take it. After two days, I was offered a handful of part-time jobs and accepted my three favorites.

One interview I'll never forget. The place was a New Age store, and my interviewer was Sylvia. Our rapport was instant, and our dialogue was short.

As I rose to leave, she shook her head and chuckled. "We're all coming together again."

"Who?" I questioned.

She looked me dead in the eye. "Those of us who were accused as witches."

Her psychic insight was right on the money. She became a close friend overnight, and although she'd hinted at a past life as a witch, I didn't press the subject. Still, I found it interesting that she'd also dealt with the specter of false accusation in her current life. Her experience was as grim as mine, but in many ways, we'd had it easier this time around.

Intuition can strike at any time. Where past lives are concerned, travel—exposure to new places and cultures—can start it buzzing.

During a trip to Ireland at age twenty-six, I booked a day trip to Connemara on impulse. The highlight was Kylemore Abbey, a nineteenth-century castle—with battlements and all—that Benedictine nuns ran as a girls' boarding school. I drank in the beauty of the lakeside walk, but as I approached the Neo-Gothic chapel, a strange thought popped into my head.

No. It's too new.

The sacred atmosphere of the abbey felt right. Connecting the experience to modern structures didn't.

I blinked, then rolled my eyes. By American standards, Kylemore Abbey was old. What was I thinking?

Perhaps that was the point: I wasn't thinking; I was feeling. My intuition spoke loud and clear.

Later in the week, I was in Killarney. On my own, I sought out the ruins of the fifteenth-century Franciscan monastery of Irrelagh (*Oir Bhealach*), now referred to as Muckross Abbey. It was dinnertime, and even the most dogged tourists had left the grounds. Still, I felt compelled to go there.

I followed the dirt path through the graveyard and entered what had been the nave of the church. Then I made my way to the cloister courtyard. The centerpiece of the small quadrangle was a large yew tree that was supposed to be as old as the abbey itself.

Now this feels right, I thought. *Not the place, but the time.*

I climbed the spiral steps of every stairwell, explored the empty rooms, and checked the views from each window slit. Then I returned to the courtyard, sat on the cold stone floor, and closed my eyes. I intended to rest only a minute, but the whispering wind lulled me to sleep.

I'm not sure what woke me, but I'd been asleep for quite some time. The sun had begun its descent, and the abbey walls darkened, as though eaten by the long shadows that crept along the ancient stone.

Except for the great yew tree, I was alone. A sudden gust of air whistled down a deserted corridor. It was the only sound— besides the scuffing of my boots as I stood—that touched the stone skeleton that had once been an abbey.

Its flesh and lifeblood were long gone, but as I turned toward a winding stairwell, I froze. I could've sworn I'd glimpsed a solemn, robed figure disappearing up the steps.

Oddly, I felt no fear. If a monk's ghost was about, he was my sacred brother, for I knew at the core of my being that I, too, had lived a monastic life. Not in that abbey, but in another.

The atmosphere of Kylemore Abbey related to two lifetimes in which I was a Benedictine nun. As for Muckross Abbey, I resonated with its ambiance and age because of a life as a Franciscan nun in fifteenth-century Ireland. Intuition guided me every step of the way. In matters of Spirit, the heart and gut eclipse the intellect. Linear thinking is limited. Context and connection rule.

Pay attention to your psychic senses of clairvoyance, clairaudience, clairsentience, claircognizance, and intuition. They'll help you broaden your perspective and give you a wealth of past-life clues.

3

CHILDHOOD: FIRST INDICATIONS

So you've decided you want to learn more about your past lives. Where do you begin? Start by looking for telltale clues from your childhood.

All children are psychic. It's not something to fear, suppress, or label. It simply is what it is: natural. Children are still acclimated to the spirit world and adjusting to the physical one, so their awareness of higher dimensions and other realities is greater than most adults'. Their intuition flows without restraint.

Although it may seem like eons ago, you were once a child. That means you were aware of things you might ignore or dismiss today. Think back to your childhood. What were your favorite books, games, and toys? Perhaps you gravitated toward certain subjects.

Remember the names of your stuffed animals and dolls. If you wrote stories, the plot, location, and main characters could also be clues to past lives. So could vivid or recurring dreams about other times and places.

Did you ever feel like your name should be different from what it was? If so, what name did you prefer? Maybe you sensed a friend or family member should have a different relationship to you: a sister who seemed more like a daughter, an uncle who was more like a brother, or a friend who might've been your mother.

Several times, my neighbor's three-year-old daughter struggled against her mother and said, "No, I want my real mother!" She was referring to her mother from a past life, and the phenomenon is more common than you'd think. Perhaps you felt or claimed something similar as a child. If you feel comfortable doing so, ask childhood friends, siblings, cousins, parents, and other family members if any such moments occurred.

You might also ask them if you ever used odd expressions or words from foreign languages as a child. Ask if you told stories or made comments that could've referred to a past life. You can also pick their brains about any "bizarre" behavior you exhibited, such as over-the-top reactions to stimuli or strange preferences. Maybe you preferred spicy foods while the rest of your family stuck to bland fare. Perhaps you bowed to others when you first met them instead of shaking their hand as you were taught to do.

If you were one of the many children who see and sense spirits, think back to those experiences. Angels and spirit guides often make appearances at children's bedsides or watch them while they play. However, spirit visitors can also be loved ones from other lives, and some actually serve as spirit guides.

Did you have an irrational fear that you eventually outgrew? In many such cases, past-life trauma is a contributing factor. A child who becomes hysterical when asked to board a cruise ship might've spent her last moments of another life on a sinking ship. A child who is afraid of enclosed places, who removes even sheets and blankets from his bed so that he won't be "trapped," might've been buried alive. Night terrors are a dead giveaway of past-life ordeals rehashed. Phobias that begin at a specific age sometimes coincide with the age at which a traumatic event occurred in a past life. Parents must tread carefully around their children's fears, because they're not always imaginary.

My own childhood was rife with past-life clues. When I was three, my maternal grandfather decided to record my voice on tape, and he asked me to tell a story. My response was high-pitched and immediate.

"Once upon a time, there was a witch. But she was a good witch…"

At that point, I hadn't seen *The Wizard of Oz* or read the book, so they'd had no influence. And let's face it: most fairy-tales demonize witches, so the likelihood that I'd heard of a good one was slim. Yet I stressed my witch's virtue with passion and without hesitation.

Also as a child, I used the term "greedy-gut" several times, and since no one in my family had heard the expression before I used it, it became a catchword they associated with me. Greedy-gut is a rather old-fashioned term some Brits use to denote a glutton. But to me, a greedy-gut was no glutton; it was a person up to no good.

While consulting an encyclopedia when I was twelve, I discovered that my older brother, Billy, and I share an intriguing connection. His birthday (February 1) and mine (April 30), as well as my favorite holiday (Halloween), are all pagan sabbats: Imbolc and the eves of Beltane and Samhain, respectively. In Germany, my birthday is known as *Walpurgisnacht,* when witches allegedly gathered on the highest peak of the Harz Mountains to mark the coming of spring.

I was raised a Christian. Heck, my father was the organist and choir director of the Episcopal Church and an organist for the Catholic Church. Many Sundays, we did double duty. I even sang in a Baptist choir for four years.

None of that mattered as I stared down at the encyclopedia. My apparent link to the practice of magic thrilled me. I couldn't account for my reaction, but soon my gaze softened and my mind stilled. Absolute calm and a sense of destiny embraced me.

Of course, I thought. *It makes perfect sense.*

I jerked back to full consciousness, but my previous thought still lingered. The reason behind it was foggy, but the sense of "rightness" remained.

Years later as a senior in college, I worked on a comparative study of German and English perceptions of witchcraft in the sixteenth and seventeenth centuries. I pored over source material such as the *Malleus Maleficarum* ("The Hammer of Witches") and *Daemonologie*. My blood boiled as I read endless lies born of ignorance, prejudice, and fear. My head cautioned that I was taking the material too much to heart; that same heart cried out for justice and tolerance.

Then one night, I came across an English drawing from 1647 that depicted the seventeenth-century Witchfinder General, Matthew Hopkins, interrogating a woman about her familiars (spirits with whom she worked magic). Something about the picture made me squirm in my chair, but I read on.

After the woman endured four nights of enforced sleep deprivation, the accused shouted out the names of her helpers. Among them was Griezzell Greedigutt, a familiar who supposedly appeared to her as an imp (a mischievous fairy or demon, according to folklore).

My childhood story about the good witch, my use of the term "greedy-gut," and my reaction to the pagan link to my birthdate were suggestive. Years later, I learned they were early clues to a life in seventeenth-century England in which I healed others and was accused of witchcraft.

My childhood offered clues to other past lives, one of which concerned Scotland and Iceland. To begin with, I loved thunderstorms, even as a toddler. I also preferred leaden skies and what little cold Florida offered. The one time it snowed—without sticking, of course—I felt as though I'd won the lottery, for I coveted northern winters. No one could explain it, especially since the rest of my family lived for sunshine. To this day, when chill winds and clouds abound, my parents say it's a

"Judy day." My passionate attachment to such weather only strengthened over time, and it generated a sense of longing that encompassed not just the forecast but a forgotten place and time just beyond conscious memory.

I still recall the sense of destiny and nostalgia that accompanied my introduction to "The Skye Boat Song" in elementary school. The lyrics (not the traditional ones, but those written by Robert Louis Stevenson) touched me deeply, and I felt that they described not just a place, but a "lost" part of my soul. I envisioned another life, not as a lad but a lass. It would be years before I traveled to Scotland, but in my mind's eye, I saw windswept, sloping mountains, lakes and seas as gray as the blessed clouds above them, and a chain of misty islands that were somehow important to me. Tears blurred my vision, and I blinked them away so my classmates and music teacher wouldn't see the effect the song had on me. Both the lyrics and the tune spoke to me of "home."

A related memory concerns the actor Leif Garrett, who was a teen heartthrob when I was a child. I wasn't a teen yet, and his image—plastered on innumerable magazines—did nothing for my heart. His name, however, did. I vividly remember a visit to my cousins' house during which I insisted that the actor's name should be pronounced "Layf," not "Leaf."

"How do you know?" they asked.

"I don't know," I answered. "I just do."

A decade later, I spent my junior year of college at the University of Aberdeen in Scotland. The move felt right, and I soaked up the beauty and romance of auld lang syne. The biggest change involved my dreams. Out of nowhere, I gained the ability to discern whether a dream was "only a dream" or contained real information. Sometimes I knew while the dream was in progress; other times I woke with a deep conviction that it was important. If I awoke at precisely 3:00 am, it was a premonition.

I relished living on the North Sea, but from the moment I arrived in Scotland, I longed to visit the Western Isles. As luck—or fate—would have it, one of my flatmates, Alison, hailed from the Hebridean Isle of Barra, and she became a friend for life. She invited me home to the Hebrides for spring break, and we visited Barra and the adjacent Vatersay, as well as the place I'd yearned to visit since elementary school, the Isle of Skye (Norse: *skuy*, "misty isle," or *skýey* or *skuyö*, "isle of cloud"). From the moment we boarded the ferry, an overpowering sense of rightness warmed my heart. I was supposed to be there. Why, I didn't know, but it was as clear to me as a mountain stream.

That night, in our Kyleakin bed and breakfast, I dreamed. A woman watched me from the far corner of a room where I lay abed. I was supposed to be sleeping, but I knew she was there. Her greed was palpable. She wanted something of mine, badly enough to pretend I was welcome in her home. Slowly, inexorably, she crept toward my bed.

I woke with a start and squinted at each corner of the tiny room. Alison shifted in the bed opposite me and mumbled something in her sleep. Her positive presence calmed my nerves, but as I nestled against my pillow, the memory of the dream swelled.

Who was the watcher in the shadows? What did she want? I had the sense we'd been on a farm, far from Skye. I somehow belonged to the Western Isles of Scotland; the woman did not. Anything more was supposition, and in the interest of sleep, I left it alone.

More than two decades later, I honed in on what I knew was a past life in both Scotland and Iceland, though I couldn't make the connection. All of a sudden, I recalled my trip to Barra. At the time, I also wanted to travel to the Hebridean Isle of Tiree, but for some reason, Alison and I didn't go. Why? Were there no ferries between the two islands?

Simply out of curiosity, I typed "Barra" into the search engine. The first website I checked showed the image of a lymphad, the ancient, single-masted galley found in Scottish heraldry... and in the dream I'd had in Cork so many years earlier! The symbol appears in the Western Isles Council flag *and* in the Chief of Clan Sinclair's coat of arms. This information seemed significant, because Alison's surname was Sinclair. Had my dream alerted me to future events, when I would meet her and see the islands myself? Was it connected to a past life in the Hebrides?

I checked into ferry schedules. Travel between Barra and Tiree was only available on Thursdays. Thursday... my favorite day of the week since childhood because I liked the way the word sounded and the pleasant feel of teeth on tongue when I pronounced it. For the first time, I made the connection between my lifelong love of thunderstorms and the fact that my favorite day of the week was named after the thunder god, Thor.

I read on. The ferry from Barra to Tiree passed the islet of Gunna.

"Gunna," I said aloud, and it seemed familiar. "Thor and Gunna. Thorgunna?"

I frowned. Then I threw caution to the wind and googled "Thorgunna," just to see if it was a real name.

It was. A woman of noble birth named Thorgunna lived in the tenth century and gave birth to a son named Thorgils, the only child of Leifr Eiríksson.

Leif Eriksson? *The* Leif Eriksson?

Leif, the son of Erik the Red, was born in Iceland. While still a lad, his father killed a man during the Althing, an annual summer meeting of leaders from all over Iceland. Erik was banished from Iceland for three years. He sailed to the west and came upon a new land, which he named Greenland, and it became the family's home.

Dan and I had long wanted to travel to Greenland but hadn't yet made the trip. We did travel to Iceland, though, the winter before our wedding. It was our first overseas trip together. While there, we felt powerfully drawn to Þingvellir, the site of the Althing from 930 until 1844, and we took a bus tour to Skálholt, one of the most important religious centers in Iceland and an episcopal see (the official seat of bishops) from 1056. As the bus slowed to a halt, an unexpected sense of urgency gripped me. I had to stand on that patch of ground. Not alone, but with Dan at my side. The two of us together, as one.

Hand in hand, we climbed the stairs and stood in front of the cathedral. I closed my eyes, took a deep breath, and let it out. Then relief flooded through me. I felt as though Dan and I had done something we were meant to do, like we'd both made good on a promise. What that promise was, I couldn't say. I only knew we'd done something positive by going there together.

I continued my research. As an adult, Leif set off on a voyage to Norway. En route, a storm supposedly blew him off course to the Isle of Tiree, which, like most of the Scottish islands at that time, was under Norse control. One source stated that the day he arrived, a storm came in and prevented his departure for a month.

Tiree was Thorgunna's home. She was known to embroider tapestries and predict the future, even the weather. Before Leif left for Norway, Thorgunna revealed she was pregnant and foresaw that the child would be a boy. She evidently told Leif that she and the boy would journey to Greenland one day.

A memory stirred. My prophetic dreams—the ones linked to 3:00 am—began right when I moved to Scotland. Was that change sparked by my proximity to Thorgunna's Tiree? After all, she had the gift of prophecy, and that gift basically dropped in my lap once I arrived. In addition, it seemed too coincidental that the flatmate who became one of my dearest friends was from Barra, the southernmost inhabited island of the Outer Hebrides and the closest of those islands to Tiree. Did my studies in Scotland serve not only to educate me but also to fulfill my soul's hidden desire to connect with Thorgunna? Had I known her in a past life?

Nantucket, an inner voice urged. *Find the connection between Leif and Nantucket.*

I wasn't aware there was a connection but decided to check it out. It turned out that Leif sailed to Newfoundland, Nova

Scotia, and on to New England. Not only was he thought to have visited Nantucket, but it was possible he named the place *Nauticon*, a Norse approximation of the original Native American name for the Island, *Natocket*.

Dan and I lived on Nantucket for exactly one year. When we moved there, I was five months pregnant and big as a whale, prompting jokes about the return of Moby-Dick. But all joking ceased once my new doctor informed us that multiple births were impossible on the island.

Our twins would have to be delivered in Boston. To make matters worse, the likelihood of premature birth meant my moving to Boston six weeks before the due date. Dan would have to stay on the island and work, and I was terrified he wouldn't be there for the births.

As it happened, I went into labor two days before I was scheduled to go to Boston. Dan stayed right by my side—from the flight to the mainland to the day we first visited the boys in the NICU (neonatal intensive care unit). Leif was long gone when Thorgunna gave birth to their son, but Dan was definitely there for me!

Back to the research. Typing "Thorgunna" into the search engine pulled up a number of articles, several of which described a story from one of the Icelandic histories, the *Eyrbyggja Saga*. It featured an older Hebridean woman named Thorgunna, and although nothing I read linked her with Leif's Thorgunna, I couldn't help but connect them.

Apparently, this Thorgunna arrived one summer at Snaefellness, Iceland, on a boat from Dublin manned by Irish and Hebrideans. Her shipmates—some of them Norsemen—reported that she possessed luxurious bedding, tapestries, and other finery not to be found in Iceland. When a Froda house-wife named Thurid (or Thurida) heard of it, she went to the boat and asked to see Thorgunna's treasures. Thorgunna obliged but refused to sell her possessions, so Thurid invited her to stay at her farm. To earn her keep, Thorgunna chose to work at the loom and in the fields rather than sell the items Thurid continued to covet.

In the fall—the night after a freak storm supposedly rained blood onto the hay fields—Thorgunna fell ill. Certain that death approached, she called Thurid's husband to her bedside and asked him to arrange for her burial and the disposal of her property. She directed him to burn her bed with its fine coverlet and hangings and to deliver her corpse to Skálholt, for she presaged it would become one of the most famous Christian centers in the land.

When Thorgunna died, Thurid prevented her husband from burning the bedclothes, after which a "weird-moon" (described as a specter or meteor shaped as a half-moon) flew around their home every night for a week. This "wonder" was thought to signal the imminent death of a family member, and when eighteen members of the household died—followed by nightly apparitions of the dead—Thurid's contempt for Thorgunna's last wishes was blamed.

Meanwhile, the corpse bearers kept their promise, and on the one occasion when a farmer withheld from them his hospitality, Thorgunna's ghost appeared to ensure he made them welcome. Finally, they arrived at Skálholt, and Thorgunna's body was laid to rest … respectfully, but without family or friends to bid her farewell.

Was there truly a connection between us? If so, it could clarify the meaning of my dream of the lurking, greedy woman while on the Isle of Skye. It might also explain the relief and gratitude that surged through me at Skálholt when Dan stood by my side. This older Thorgunna traveled to Iceland on a boat that originated in Dublin, and I'd dreamed of such a boat and a tenth-century Hiberno-Norse penny that was minted in Dublin.

These are only some of the connections I've made to that long-ago life. Looking back at my childhood, the clues to that lifetime are crystal clear. That's why you should search your own childhood. It could lead you to countless connections and a new understanding about your past and present realities.

OTHER CHILDREN'S OBSERVATIONS

Your childhood memories are only part of the equation. Children you know currently could surprise you with information about past lives. When dealing with your own children—who likely played and/or are playing roles in several of your lives—the plot thickens. Pay particular attention to impromptu information, drawings, and the use of foreign words.

Impromptu Information

Children ask questions that leave you tongue-tied. On occasion, they drop bombs of information right in your lap.

One day when my boys were five, we were driving down the road. Out of nowhere, Geoffrey said, "We don't live in England anymore."

I looked at him through the mirror. "Who are you talking about?" I asked.

"Our family," he answered. "We live in Florida, not England."

"We're not in outer space either," Connor chimed in. "We're back on Earth."

Dan and I shared a meaningful glance, but the boys dropped the subject.

Later that day, while the boys were playing, a faraway look touched Connor's face. "We have to watch out for the bridge, Mommy," he said.

"What bridge?" I questioned.

He clammed up and continued playing. But more information was forthcoming.

At bedtime, after Geoffrey had donned his pajamas, he sat beside me on his bed. "Mommy," he said, "in a past life, everybody thought you were evil. You weren't, but they thought so. So they bullied you. But everybody loves you now."

Dumbfounded, I stared at him. His face took on the same look that Connor's had earlier.

"We have to be really careful around the bridge," he continued. "There was a man and a girl. The girl jumped off, and then the man. They both died. Remember that?"

After a moment, I found my tongue.

"No, honey. When was this?"

"A while ago. The girl had a string hanging from her neck."

He cocked his head to the side and pulled his hand out and away from his neck, as though pulling on a rope.

A hangman's noose, I thought. *And a scaffold looks like a bridge.*

The pictorial image of the seventeenth-century Witch-finder General, Matthew Hopkins, flooded my vision. A moment later, it wavered and was replaced by an ex-boyfriend's face. I hadn't thought of him in years, but suddenly I knew. In a past life, he was Matthew Hopkins. How this fact had escaped my intuition for so long boggled the mind. I knew he'd accused me of witchcraft in a past life, but until that moment, his actual identity had been a mystery. I can only guess that the connection touched on events so painful, I held them at bay for as long as possible. But my children's observations about that life brought everything to a head and helped me face it.

Not long afterward, the boys came out with information suggestive of another past life. They came up behind me while I was reading a book on haunted royal homes. One page had a picture of Hampton Court Palace in England.

"That looks like a castle," Geoffrey said.

"No," said Connor. "It's a palace."

A picture of Cardinal Wolsey was also visible.

"Was he a king?" Geoffrey asked, pointing.

"No," Connor said immediately. "He wasn't a king."

Then Geoffrey turned the page, and a portrait of Henry VIII stared back at us.

"I've seen him before," Geoffrey said. "I know him. I think he was a king."

Connor spoke in a strong, matter-of-fact tone. "He lived in the palace and had the power to destroy his enemies."

Neither boy had seen information about Tudor England on TV. Lost for words, I stared at the king's picture. Then I felt a gentle touch on the back of my head. Connor was caressing my hair.

Slowly, I turned to him. Love and compassion shimmered in his beautiful brown eyes, and I wondered just how much he knew about a life we had shared in sixteenth-century England.

Children's observations can involve other people, too: friends, family, teachers, etc. In the moment, deflect any embarrassment you might feel and roll with it. Not only could you learn about another person's past life, but that lifetime could be connected to you.

About a month after the boys started preschool, the school nurse phoned me. Connor and Geoffrey had collided with each other on the playground, and although Geoffrey was fine, Connor was having trouble supporting himself on his left leg. It was the same leg that he'd clutched during several night terrors while screaming, "My leg! It hurts! Someone help my leg!"

Ten minutes later, I rushed into the school office. Connor's eyes lit up when he saw me. He started forward, dragging his left foot behind him. After a few steps, his knee buckled.

I raced toward him and hugged him with all of my might. Then I pulled back to gauge his expression and asked him what had happened.

He looked me dead in the eye, smiled, and pointed to the side of his neck. "Neck," he said.

I've got to get him to the chiropractor, I thought.

When Dan showed up, he also asked Connor what had happened.

Connor pointed to the same spot as before. "Neck," he repeated.

Listen to your intuition, an inner voice advised. *Get him to the chiropractor.*

As it turned out, our chiropractor immediately pinpointed the source of the trouble: the top vertebra in Connor's neck, aka the atlas. Apparently, Connor had fallen just right on his tailbone so the impact traveled up his spine and knocked his atlas out of place. It was both twisted and tilted, causing the sacrum and L5 vertebra in his lower back to twist and pinch a nerve associated with the L5. Connor's dragging and buckling left leg was what chiropractors call "drop foot."

The doctor adjusted Connor's neck, which corrected the L5 and relieved pressure from the nerve. Two minutes later, Connor hopped off the table and walked normally out of the office.

After his teachers witnessed his immediate recovery, we had a chat with his favorite teacher, Ms. C. She mentioned a storybook they used to teach the parts of the body. Every time they reached the part about the neck, even if someone else was reading the book, Connor would approach Ms. C and put his hands on her neck. Connor always seemed to know when my atlas was out of whack, so I asked if she had neck problems.

"There's a certain bone on the back of my neck that sticks out," she answered. "Whenever I push on it, I get an instant headache."

I knew from past experience that both of my boys were sensitive to energy, including chakras and auras. Still, I couldn't help wondering if Connor's sense about our necks had as much to do with a past life as with his sensitivity. I later learned that both Ms. C and I had been beheaded in another life, and Connor was a part of that lifetime.

Drawings

Children's drawings can give you a wealth of past-life information. When my boys were four, Geoffrey drew a picture of two people aboard what looked like a Viking ship in a storm. One person was a woman with long hair; the other was a man wearing a conical hat.

When I asked him what the drawing depicted, he replied, "The first time we met. But I need to put Indian stuff in it too."

He proceeded to draw a man with something resembling feathers in his hair at the front of the boat looking toward the horizon. Between the "Indian" and the man who was supposed to be Geoffrey, he drew a huge being with numerous large feathers. It seemed to be either an animal or a person wearing a ceremonial costume. Because it towered over everyone else in the boat, it could've been a spirit.

The combination of Norse and Native American elements immediately brought to mind the boys' twinspeak. Out of what seemed a sizable vocabulary—which included sounds not present in the English language—Dan and I half-deciphered one word, and that was because each boy independently pointed to a large group of energetic carp in the zoo's fish tank and pronounced, "*Beo*."

Maybe *beo* was just their word for fish, but my research yielded three suggestive tidbits: (1) in Irish, *beo* is a noun meaning "living thing" or "livelihood" and an adjective meaning "lively" or "active"; (2) in Breton, *beo* is an obsolete form of *bev*, "having life," related to *beva*, which means "to live" or "to feed"; (3) in Newfoundland, the Vikings traded with Native Americans known as the Beothuk, who were avid fishermen.

To me, it begged the question: how do infant twins create their twinspeak? Is it a testament to human imagination and ingenuity? Sure. But it's possible that twins draw a portion of their vocabulary from other lifetimes they've shared—or are sharing, since all time is now. Perhaps they access a massive spectrum of memories and languages to gather a miraculous miscellany of associated words for their private, one-of-a-kind language. Twinspeak could be living, linguistic proof of the soul's immortality. And the word *beo* just might point to a lifetime in which the Norse and Native American cultures intersected, just as they seemed to connect in Geoffrey's drawing.

Foreign Words

The previous account stresses the role that language—even a single word—can play in past-life discovery. Not everyone will encounter twinspeak, but on occasion, you may hear a child use a word or two from another language. Try not to jump to conclusions, and consider sources other than past lives: something the child saw on TV, heard in a popular song, or learned from a person who knows that language. When you've exhausted all other possibilities, you'll know it's a past-life clue.

When our boys turned three, Dan and I gave them a cardboard version of a fifteenth-century castle, complete with paper noblemen, vassals, and accessories like shields and swords. Geoffrey grabbed a sword and brandished it in the air. Then he aimed it at me and looked straight into my eyes.

"*Fendre, fendre,*" he said.

His pronunciation of the "r" sounded French, and I heard that particular "r" in the boys' twinspeak from time to time.

But the only French word I knew that sounded remotely similar was *fenêtre*.

He continued to wave the paper sword in the air. "*Fendre*, Mommy! *Fendre*," he repeated with a glint in his eye.

When he turned his attention to Connor, I scurried to the bookshelf and seized a French-English dictionary. After a brief search, I found the word. The definition was perfect: "to cut through; to cleave in two."

Even more intriguing was Geoffrey's pronunciation of the word, which was quite different from what a modern French speaker would say. He pronounced *fendre* as it would've been spoken hundreds of years ago.

One morning, months later, Geoffrey's face took on that familiar faraway look I'd come to recognize as a moment of vision. Then he turned to me.

"Mommy," he said, "you're like an angel, and I love you. We were reborn, but I don't want to remember my other lifetimes right now."

"But I want to," Connor said without missing a beat. "You and daddy were knights, Geoffrey."

A couple years later, I spoke with the same psychic team I mentioned earlier, and they revealed that I'd known Geoffrey during a life in pre-Renaissance France when he was a knight at the French court. There was some connection to the city of Lyons (Lyon), and apparently, he had loved me from afar in the fashion of courtly love. The psychics' revelation helped to explain the clues I'd gathered up till then and why Geoffrey was sometimes possessive of my affections.

Revisit your childhood and really listen to the children who surround you today. You never know what tidbit will jump-start an investigation or confirm information about another life. If the subject of psychic children interests you or you suspect your own child is psychic, check out the recommended reading list at the back of this book for titles that can help you explore this area further.

4

INSTINCTIVE REACTIONS

Inexplicable reactions to—or strong emotions associated with—locations, landscapes, weather, décor, cultures, languages, traditions, professions, animals, objects, symbols, tastes, smells, music, and other sounds can point to past-life connections. The more intense the reaction or emotion is, the greater the indication.

ATTRACTION

Attraction that's associated with past lives isn't merely an interest; it's a compulsion that sometimes borders on obsession. For example, you've always wanted to travel to a specific city or country, or perhaps the location never entered your mind until a sudden and recent urge struck you. This desire has nothing to do with a friend or relative having gone there or anything romantic you might've heard about the place. You just know you have to go there, even if you've no idea why, and your determination is unshakable.

Such cases demonstrate the soul's desire to reunite with another piece of itself. Your arrival at the location might spark a full-blown memory of a moment from your past—actually, another "present" into which you've tapped—or the integration could happen on a subtler level. Regardless, the reunion is another step forward on your spiritual path. I've experienced this type of attraction many times, but one of the strongest pulls I ever felt was toward Ireland.

One night in the summer before my senior year of high school, I kicked off my bedcovers with a vengeance. I'd been fidgeting for almost two hours, and sleep remained a stranger. I yearned for something I couldn't name and had the curious feeling that I should be doing something. Exactly what, I had no clue, but I rolled my eyes, abandoned my bed, and made my way to the living room.

I scanned the bookshelves for several minutes until my gaze locked on a book I'd never noticed before: *Ireland: A Picture Book to Remember Her By*. Intrigued, I grabbed it and settled on the couch.

From the moment I opened the book, I changed. Waves of emotion rushed over me: love, sorrow, and, strangest of all, homesickness. Gratitude flooded my heart and mind, for this was what I'd been seeking. I turned each page with reverence, melding my being with the images thereon.

It was crazy. I was born and raised in blazingly hot Florida, about as far from Ireland and its blissfully cool climate as one could get. Before that night, I'd never considered the

Emerald Isle. Now my whole life seemed to have led me to the discovery that I was linked to that distant land.

Desire and will swelled within me. I jumped up and raced to my parents' bedroom. With dispatch, I woke them and broke the news. Come hell or high water, I was going to Ireland.

My parents didn't know what to make of my new obsession, but the next morning, my father informed me that my great-grandfather had emigrated from Ireland in 1914. How this fact had escaped my notice for seventeen years was beyond me, but now that I knew of my Irish heritage, I was unstoppable.

My enthusiasm for Ireland was contagious, and by senior graduation, three round-trip plane tickets lay on my parents' desk. My parents and I were bound for Shannon Airport.

Excitement forbade sleep on the long flight over, so after we'd shuffled through customs, traded dollars for pounds, and procured our rental car, we drove straight to our bed and breakfast in the village of Bunratty and took a nap. When I awoke hours later, my mother had some news: she'd heard me speaking Irish Gaelic in my sleep.

"How do you know?" I asked.

Her answer was a carbon copy of my little brother's and my standard explanation for any moment we became infused with knowledge as children. "I just know."

I believed her, for several reasons. She's honest to a fault, and she picks up languages the way toddlers pick up forbidden, germ-ridden objects off the ground. Furthermore, she's always had a way of knowing things that by logic, she shouldn't. Her mother shared this ability.

My own instincts implored me to pay attention. From the moment I stepped foot on Irish soil, I felt I'd come home. This was no shallow sentiment; it was a gut reaction, a re-union with a piece of my soul.

Maybe my Irish speech was a monologue. Maybe it was part of a dialogue with someone my mother couldn't see. Either way, its impact on my beliefs was significant. Reincarnation now seemed as credible and natural as the cyclic return of spring.

Ireland's landscape was as gorgeous as its people were gracious, but my response to its beauty seemed greatest in Killarney. There, while bouncing in the back of a jaunting cart, I became one with my surroundings. The cool wind caressed my cheeks and whipped my long, blond hair into a wild mass that would've made any banshee proud. Low-hanging purple clouds harmonized with rippling lakes, and the gentle slope of mountains accompanied them. Flowering bushes, rustling trees, and fertile soil moist with promise completed the symphony. Each note had perfect pitch. Every phrase was pure magic.

When our driver reined in his horse, my parents jumped from the cart, eager to tour Muckross House. I shared their enthusiasm but was so caught up in nature's melody, I didn't want the ride to end. Still, history summoned me, so I followed their lead and strode toward the house.

Abruptly, I hesitated. The lake to my right seemed familiar, and the adjacent parkland beckoned. But I had to resist its pull. An amble through the woods would never fit into our jam-packed schedule.

At a future date, I would explore those woods and discover a surprising piece to add to my life's puzzle. That night, my mother heard me speak Irish in my sleep once more.

Another facet of attraction is that you and important people from your past lives become, in a sense, living, breathing magnets. A telltale sign of this phenomenon is someone drawn to the same city or workplace as you around the same time. I've experienced this phenomenon on a number of occasions. The other person—or you—and/or the location act as a temporary magnet switched on at the proper time. For example, the boys' beloved teacher, Ms. C, and her family moved to Florida at the same time we did. Not only did they play important roles in our current lifetime, but we were all connected in at least three other lifetimes—one in Egypt and two in England.

I've experienced past-life magnetism many times, but the most life-changing instance involved my husband, Dan. I first met him (in this life) at age thirty-one when I traveled to Williamsburg, Virginia. I'd been there twice before and sensed it would be my home one day. That day had arrived, so I flew into Newport News and gave myself one week to find a job at Colonial Williamsburg and a place to live.

With dispatch, I achieved both objectives. Then I celebrated with a leisurely evening in the historic area, wholly unaware I had a date with destiny and a man I'd known centuries before in Ireland.

It was 4:45 in the afternoon as I schlepped along DOG (Duke of Gloucester) Street. Swimming in sweat, I squinted up at the glaring summer sun. For a minute, I thought I was going to pass out. Then I spied a divine stretch of shade beneath the entrance to the eighteenth-century courthouse and made a beeline for it.

A young man in colonial garb with wavy, brown hair and blue-gray eyes guarded the door. I must've looked pathetic, because he grinned as I approached.

We remarked on the hellish heat, shook hands, and introduced ourselves as Dan and Judy. Then we settled into an easy conversation, and I learned he was a native of New Jersey and only recently employed at Colonial Williamsburg.

He told me his parents had honeymooned there and had taken him to Williamsburg on vacation when he was a boy. He'd fallen in love with the place, and a couple of months ago, the urge to return and serve the Colonial Williamsburg Foundation had seized him, just as it had me.

It quickly became apparent that with minimal adjustments to time and circumstance, we might have met before. He'd studied in England during college, just as I had, and he'd flown into Heathrow just weeks after I'd come and gone through the same airport. Heathrow is huge, but the fact that we'd been drawn to England within weeks of each other is notable.

A couple years later, during the time I lived in Salem, he traveled to Boston on business. On impulse, he visited Salem and found his way to my friend Sylvia's New Age store, where I used to work. I wasn't there that day, but the fact that he was is remarkable because of one key point: before that day, he'd all but ignored metaphysics and the paranormal.

Now, we'd both been drawn to Williamsburg. A week after our first meeting, I was again in the historic area, climbing the stairs of the restored Magazine to view the weapons display on the second floor. While staring at a British flag, I zoned out.

All of a sudden, I thought of Dan. *Where are you, Dan?* I asked in my mind.

I glanced at the door and started toward it, as though pulled. Without knowing why, I marched down the stairs and out of the Magazine. Then I crossed DOG Street and the Courthouse green in a straight line that led right to the Randolph House.

There he was in eighteenth-century costume, guarding the gate against a long line of tourists. Somehow I'd answered my own question and known where to go. Or perhaps a part of Dan had "heard" my question and responded on a level of which neither of us was consciously aware.

But I didn't waste time pondering the point. Instead, I started toward him and stopped two feet away.

"You probably don't remember me, but I'm Judy," I said.

By some miracle, he did remember me. Even more miraculous was my timing; I had arrived right at his break time. As if on cue, another costumed interpreter appeared to take his place.

Dan and I strolled away from the house, then down Nicholson Street toward the Cabinetmaker. Casual observers might well have mistaken us for longtime friends. As for me, I had a gut feeling we were meant to meet. It had nothing to do with romance. It simply felt right to walk beside him, and I knew on some level, I'd chosen to do so.

Repulsion

Repulsion, which can manifest as a sudden or inexplicable phobia, often indicates a past-life incident—or a part of your soul—you'd rather forget. When I was eight years old, a snake phobia hit me seemingly overnight. I'd never had a problem with snakes before, but suddenly, if I happened upon pictures of them in books or magazines, I freaked out. Even cartoon images made me uncomfortable.

Years later, I met with a gifted psychic in the spiritualist community of Cassadaga, Florida. I questioned her about a number of things, including the source of my snake phobia.

Her eyes closed, and she gave me a running commentary of her clairvoyant vision. "I see you as a little girl in another life. You're wearing a blue Victorian dress, standing in a large yard behind a massive house. You see a snake slithering in the grass at your feet, but you're not afraid. You're just curious. You reach down to touch it, and it bites you. You stagger a little and fall. A woman—it feels like your mother—runs across the lawn, falls to her knees, and lifts you onto her lap. She calls for help and starts to cry. You die in her arms."

I recoiled at the thought that I'd touched a snake in any lifetime. But my aversion quickly turned to sympathy for the sobbing mother. I could almost see her face. I blinked hard and brushed the image aside. The psychic explained that the event occurred when my past-life self was eight years old, which is why my snake phobia appeared around the same age in this life.

My subsequent relationship with snakes has been a tricky one. I still don't like them and avoid them when I can, but I've come to realize the snake is my shadow totem. Among animal totems, the shadow totem is a guide who takes the form of an animal you initially fear but later acknowledge as an ally. Whether I'm dreaming or awake, when snakes show up, they're connected to specific messages, usually regarding transformation or healing.

In the spring of 1998, I was living in Florida with my parents and nursing my low back injury. It wasn't long before my thoughts latched on to one of the more healing places I'd visited in recent years, the Pacific Northwest. Then I remembered that one of my best friends from high school had moved to a small town outside of Tacoma, Washington. On impulse, I phoned her and booked a flight to Sea-Tac.

I stayed with her for a month, during which we laughed until our bellies hurt and rekindled our friendship with zest. Funny, then, that the trip was marked on either end by events I'd rather have skipped. Namely, two separate encounters with a snake.

Up to that point, I'd never run into one in the wild, even though I was raised in Florida. Since I couldn't handle them in pictures or movies, you'd think I would've freaked when I saw one up close. That wasn't the case.

Was I startled? Yes. Repelled? You bet. But I didn't scream, flinch, or run away, all of which suggested progress.

In the first instance, I was strolling along the sidewalk past a church when a long, thin specimen darted across my path, not two inches from my toes. The second time, I spotted a honking-huge black daddy sunning itself on the opposite side of the dirt road I trod. Needless to say, I gave it a wide berth.

To leave a place where snakes were common only to meet two in a single month in an environment where they seemed less common was compelling. In Eastern traditions, the serpent symbolizes the kundalini energy coiled at the base of the spine, which, when released, travels upward to activate energy centers associated with sexuality, creativity, and new levels of awareness. To Native Americans, the snake is a symbol of initiation, wisdom, healing, and rebirth, of ingesting a poison to transmute it.

I could certainly equate my back pain with poison, and the significance of my being injured while writing—my personal expression of creativity—wasn't lost on me. My present pain was my own creation: not only did it mimic past-life trauma, but it also represented my fear of failure. I needed to transform the experience into something valuable.

Five years later in Williamsburg—when my lower back contributed to my torturous, ten-month battle with pelvic pain—I had another encounter with a snake. Its thin body coiled three feet from where I stood, but it merely startled me. By that time, the only thing I feared was continued pain. I hoped the snake's presence, and its awareness of mine, meant I would succeed a second time in transmuting the poison (i.e., rekindled fear) I'd allowed to creep back into my life. Thankfully, I did just that.

STRONG EMOTIONS

Strong, often sudden, emotions are another indicator of past-life connections. You burst into tears at the sight of a nineteenth-century photograph of a total stranger. Your heart leaps with joy the first time you hear a foreign language spoken. A particular event or period in history—especially one about which you know little—fills you with anger or regret.

Gazing upon an ancient artifact in a museum makes you nervous or gives you chills. Such clues manifest in countless ways, often when you least expect them.

My first reading with a psychic in Cassadaga occurred during the sweltering summer between my freshman and sophomore years of college. In a small room across a tiny table, the woman in question bowed her head, said a quick prayer, then fell silent. The silence stretched into one minute, then two. I felt better acquainted with the roots of her dyed hair than with her facial features and started to suspect narcolepsy. So with more force than was necessary, I cleared my throat.

Her head shot up. Then her gaze locked with mine, and she blurted, "London! Tell me about it."

Taken aback, I filed through my brain for an intelligible response. "Well," I said, "my parents and I are planning a short trip to England and Germany this summer."

She shook her head. "No, it's more than that. I see you living in London, in this life and an earlier one."

Peace settled over me. "Somehow that doesn't surprise me," I said.

"You'll be moving to London soon. The way will come."

A month later, I was in Tallahassee, Florida, registering for FSU's fall semester. A blue flier on the nearest bulletin board caught my eye. I froze, pen in hand.

LONDON STUDIES PROGRAM, it read. SIGN UP NOW FOR SPRING SEMESTER. My heart began to pound, and adrenalin coursed through my body.

The way will come, the psychic had said. And there it was. I requested a copy of the flier and set the plan in motion.

I also learned that a history course on Tudor England would be offered that fall, and I couldn't rest until I added it to my schedule. Throughout the semester, my professor couldn't miss my enthusiasm for the subject or the passion with which I took notes during his lectures. You'd have thought the information was a matter of life and death.

The spring semester found me in London. I bonded right away with my roommates, Susan and Peggy, and a Victorian hotel in South Kensington provided us and our fellow students with classrooms, accommodations, and a baptism-by-fire acquaintance with English plumbing.

Toward the end of the semester, I went with Peggy and her boyfriend to the Tower of London. Even from a distance, the fortress was intimidating, but the creepiest part of the whole complex—for me, at least—was the Traitors' Gate. A chill coursed along my spine as we strolled past it, and it took me several minutes to shake the sensation. I wondered how many innocent people had entered the tower through that gate.

My favorite memory from the outing involved the ravens on Tower Green. They added a touch of dignity to the site of the scaffold, which was as calm as it was clean—a far cry from how it must've looked when supposed traitors were executed! The mere thought of decapitation was enough to make me queasy, yet the ravens' black, iridescent plumage soothed me. One bird, in particular, noticed my presence, and our gazes locked. He exuded intelligence, and though I couldn't say why, I felt he was male. I also had the feeling he could see right through me to deep, dark places of which even I was unaware.

How long we stared at one another, I don't know. It couldn't have been too long, because my friends were close by. But as I turned away, something akin to love squeezed my heart. I looked back—to find him still watching me—and sent him a silent good-bye. Then I walked away.

A little over a year later, I was back in England for the summer, studying at Oxford University, specifically Christ Church College. Originally known as Cardinal College, it was refounded by Henry VIII in 1532 as King Henry VIII's College and in 1546 as Christ Church. I dined each day in the Great Hall at a table overlooked by a portrait of the indomitable king. It drew my gaze every time I entered the hall, and I took to smiling at it—almost in greeting—at every meal. Ridiculous, right?

On the academic front, I wrote a paper and gave a speech in defense of Anne Boleyn, Henry VIII's second wife. The fact that she'd been accused of witchcraft seemed inevitable and made me even more committed. When I mentioned the speech to my mother, she reminded me that I was distantly related to Anne. My family knew nothing of this lineage until our Irish cousins revealed it, and it seemed a plausible—if not satisfactory—explanation for why I took Tudor history so seriously.

Two other experiences—one in Massachusetts, the other in Virginia—seemed connected. First, during my time in Salem, I spent a lazy afternoon at the Museum of Fine Arts in Boston. One quiet corner within the building felt like home: an English Tudor linenfold-paneled room. The day I visited, I had the space all to myself for a good twenty minutes, which was amazing in a museum as prominent as the MFA. The dark oak paneling, limestone fireplace, and fifteenth-century stained glass window panes were beautiful, but it wasn't until I closed my eyes that the room truly came to life.

I stood perfectly still—surrounded by oak, sheathed in whispers and stirrings just on the edge of memory—and allowed the atmosphere to soak into me. I've never been sure of whom or what I sensed, but I knew beyond a shadow of a doubt that I'd lived in Tudor England and dwelled in rooms very like that one. I can honestly say my trip to the museum was one of the most exhilarating events of my life.

The second experience happened one chilly morning in Williamsburg. As I crossed the lawn outside the historic building where I worked, a raven blocked my path. I'd never seen one there before, but it was too large to be a crow. I stopped in my tracks maybe nine feet away, and we regarded each other for a long moment.

Suddenly, another raven swooped down in front of me and landed in the grass beside the other one. It gave me a curious look, and I was surprised that neither of them seemed frightened.

"Hi," I said and took a step closer.

They held their ground, so I took another step. They stayed put, but apparently I was old news, because they turned to each other instead. I hurried around them so I wouldn't be late for work.

That was the day I shared a telling dialogue with one of my coworkers. She was a fellow seeker on the spiritual path, and our affinity made our conversation even more conspicuous than it might've been. The topic? England's Elizabeth I and her association with Mary, Queen of Scots.

One thing you must know: during my third term at the University of Aberdeen in Scotland, I wrote a paper entitled "Mary, Queen of Scots: Her Fatal Flaw." I regret it now—even though my Scottish professor gave me the highest mark—because of the severity of my criticism. I applauded Mary the woman; Mary the monarch got slammed.

Now, in Williamsburg, what began as an innocent discussion spiraled into a heated debate. I championed Elizabeth's case, and the coworker defended Mary's until a sudden and simultaneous awareness struck us. Why were we arguing about two women who'd lived centuries earlier? What was the big deal?

I told my coworker about my passionate attachment to Tudor England, and she revealed that she and her sister shared a fascination with Mary, Queen of Scots. At that point, we wondered if we all had played some role in a Tudor/Stuart past. Maybe we'd been loyal subjects—or even servants—of two different queens. Or perhaps some form of ancestral memory fueled my fierce support for Anne Boleyn and her daughter, Elizabeth.

It wasn't until April of 2009 that the mystery surrounding Tudor England was finally solved, thanks to a conversation with the renowned channeler Kim O'Neill.

She told me I was going to travel to England and have an incredible regression to a past life. She also said I'd be recalling past-life events for the rest of my life.

When I asked her to explain my connection to Tudor England, her answer was immediate. "You were Katherine Howard."

Katherine Howard. She was Anne Boleyn's first cousin and Henry VIII's fifth wife, whom he called his "rose without a thorn."

I wasn't thrilled by the idea, particularly because of the way some historians and movies have portrayed Katherine. She was the wife who might have slept around on Henry. "She's the one who was *rumored* to have slept around," Kim said pointedly. In other words, she hadn't.

Once I heard that, the puzzle fell into place. If past-life charges of malevolent witchcraft weren't enough to give me a complex about false accusation, a life as Katherine Howard certainly was!

She was beheaded at the Tower of London by order of the king. Did the raven on Tower Green somehow recognize who I'd been? Did the ravens in Williamsburg show up because I was about to reconnect with that life, in which the future Queen Elizabeth was also my cousin? Your guesses are as good as mine, but the emotions that connected me to London and to the Tudors were very real.

Sometimes strong emotions indicate not only a past life but an element—a language, a person, a place, etc.—that will help you discover other lives that may or may not have anything to do with that element. The Swedish language was such an element for me.

During my third and final term at the University of Aberdeen, the historical connection between Scandinavians and Scots sparked my interest. It was then, while leafing through a well-worn library book, that I first saw written Swedish.

The instant attraction—the sense of purpose and knowing—echoed my first encounter with the Irish picture book.

This time, however, there was no sorrow involved, only excitement and longing. I ran my fingers over the page and sounded out the words to the best of my ability.

I couldn't rest until I knew exactly how each consonant and vowel should be pronounced, so I rushed to the nearest bookstore and purchased a crash course in "Swedish for Travelers." Like a woman possessed, I thrust the tape into my unsuspecting tape recorder and tapped my foot with impatience as the English introduction droned on.

After what seemed ages, a native Swede spoke, and that first sentence might as well have been Mozart. Joy cascaded through me, and as I repeated the phrase, my lips and tongue tingled with something close to recognition. I know it sounds crazy, but it felt good to speak the words. Beyond good, and the thrill was every bit as physical as it was psychological.

At the end of term, I flew to Sweden and spent two weeks there. I resonated with everything from Midsummer celebrations to pagan legends. Names like Odin, Thor, and Freya—and the traditions they'd inspired—felt more like knowledge remembered than information learned. Similar to the Irish experience, my visit to *Sverige* was like coming home.

The Swedish language was certainly related to a Scandinavian past life, but by learning it and meeting others who spoke it, I was able to connect to three other lives in England and Germany. With hindsight, I see that when I first heard Swedish, my soul recognized it as vital to my spiritual path and rejoiced.

Notice your instinctive reactions to objects, locations, infor-mation, etc. Strong, inexplicable attraction, repulsion, and emotions can be associated with past-life experience.

5

FIRST IMPRESSIONS

We've already touched on the importance of instinctive reactions to places and things. Your reactions to people—and their impressions of you—are particularly telling. If you've never understood why you and another person continually butt heads, learning that your troubles began in a "previous" life would give you some much-needed perspective on the relationship! Your foray into past lives might also help you curb making quick judgments of other people. You might loathe something your neighbor does, but chances are, at one time or another, you did something similar in another life. What we hate most in others is sometimes a reflection of what our soul knows about ourselves.

Those closest to us—family and friends we consider kindred spirits—commonly play important roles in other lifetimes. That's not to say that you knew all of your family and friends before, but there's a good chance you did. Whether your relationship is with friends, family, coworkers, or casual acquaintances, all play a role in the karmic dance and in past-life discovery.

ATTRACTION

Often, those who attract us most, who literally draw us in, are people we've known in previous lives. You meet them "for the first time" and instantly like them. That warm, fuzzy feeling is directly linked to your "prior" interactions, which occurred/ are occurring at a different point on the space-time continuum. In many cases, they're just as attracted to you.

In the summer of 1993, I traveled to a number of coastal villages in Devon and Cornwall. In one of them, I purchased an armload of books at a harborside gift shop. The cashier grinned like Lewis Carroll's Cheshire cat as she accepted my credit card. Then she suggested I visit an astrologer who lived just up the road.

I couldn't guess whether her aim was customer referral, matchmaking, or something completely different, but I followed her directions to a refurbished seventeenth-century cottage. I stared hard at the wooden door and almost turned away. Then I rolled my eyes, raised a hand, and knocked.

A tall, thin, thirty-something man with mussed, mousy hair swung open the door. The instant our gazes locked, I sensed a connection, but necessity pulled my attention to the present moment. I offered my feeble excuse for disturbing his day, and without hesitation, he ushered me inside.

A mass of papers and books covered the desk upon which his computer perched, and they seemed to imply a thriving business. Yet I sought no astrology chart. Honestly, I didn't know what I sought, and I told him so.

He smiled, accepting my unannounced visit with aplomb, and we relaxed into an easy conversation. How long it lasted, I don't recall, but it was unguarded and heartfelt. By the time I rose to leave, I felt I'd made a friend.

I headed for the door, but when I tried to open it, the old-fashioned latch rebelled. The astrologer offered to help and came up behind me.

The warmth of his body caressed my back, and a wave of intense longing rippled through me. Unshakable conviction prickled my skin.

I know this man, I thought. *We were once lovers.*

Maybe it helped to sense him rather than see him, but there was no doubt in my heart or mind. My body agreed, for when he reached his arm around me to open the door, I shuddered. All I wanted in that moment was to fall back into his embrace.

As it happened, I stumbled out of the cottage. Decorum and logic demanded I go, so I turned and waved good-bye. My head abuzz, my nerves aflutter, I started down the road.

Sleep played hide-and-seek with me that night as I pondered my connection to the astrologer. It felt archaic, and he radiated a quiet wisdom that I somehow sensed we shared. I would've bet money that we'd known each other in England. The exact where and when remained elusive, but a bit of validation arrived in the form of a letter after I returned home. The astrologer wrote that he'd felt an immediate connection with me and suspected we'd known each other in another life. I wasn't crazy after all!

Attraction doesn't have to be romantic in nature. When I first started graduate school at the University of Wisconsin-Madison, I met a woman named Bożena. She was ten years my senior and a fellow linguistics student from Poland. From day one, we bonded, and she could've been my sister. Like me, she'd studied Swedish and German, and historical linguistics and phonetics were as pivotal in her life as in mine. Before we ever met, we'd longed to visit the same sites: Machu Picchu, Abu Simbel, and Skara Brae, to name a few. She also shared my fascination for the British Isles and Scandinavia. First and foremost, she was open to mystical exploration, and we discussed all aspects of the paranormal at length. Years later, we discovered we were closely related during a lifetime in eighth-century England and Germany. Our attraction to the same ancient, historic sites suggests other past-life connections as well.

REPULSION

Often, people who repel us are those we've dealt with in previous lives. In most cases, the repulsion is an immediate, visceral reaction. At your "first" meeting, you instantly dislike them for no apparent reason. That dose of dread is directly linked to your relationship in a "past" (i.e., simultaneous) life. You might ignore your reaction and forge a new relationship with that person, but your first impression is planted firmly in your memory.

I experienced such a meeting when I was twenty-four, but in order for you to understand its implications, I need to describe a dream I had the night before I started classes at UW-Madison.

I scurried along a dirt road, darting glances toward the forest on either side. Should I stand my ground or flee? Even now, the frenzied crowd swarmed toward me. Their grumbles and growls fought the distant thunder for supremacy over the air while I struggled to regain my composure.

Time and again, I'd used my natural gifts and herbal knowledge to help and to heal. No one complained when a headache ceased or when a lifelong wish came true. Why should they doubt me now?

Overnight, friends had become strangers. Now, as they advanced to form a half-moon around me, I regretted my years in their service.

All at once, a familiar presence reached silky, deceptive tendrils toward my back. I knew without looking who stood behind me, and he was no friend.

I whipped around to face him. His dark eyes glowed with malice beneath the wide brim of his high-crowned, black hat.

Black clothes, black heart, black soul.

The wind caught his cloak as he raised an arm and pointed at me. "Witch," he spat.

Heat flushed my cheeks. The sanctimonious, hypocritical viper! He thought he knew me. He assumed he'd won.

Very well, *I thought*. You accuse me of wielding power, but you have no idea what I could do if I willed it so. Stand back, liar. I'll show you power.

I shut my eyes and connected with the familiar energy coiled at the base of my spine. It spiraled upward and expanded until my entire body vibrated with the force of it. The power surged within me, and I prepared to strike…

I jerked upward in bed and stared at the enveloping darkness. That was no dream; it held the unmistakable resonance of memory, of truth. Our speech and clothing indicated seventeenth-century England or America. The end result for an accused witch was rarely good. In England and America, most were hanged.

Whatever the man's identity, one point was clear: I hated him with a passion I never knew I possessed. As illogical as it sounds, I hopped out of bed and checked my bathroom and closet, just to make sure he hadn't followed me into my waking world. Hours passed before I fell back asleep, and the only reason I did was because every light in my apartment was on.

Two years later, I'd earned my master's degree, but my future was still undecided. I'd been nominated for a scholarship to study at a *folkhögskola* in Forsa, Sweden, and I chose to live with my family in Florida while awaiting the decision.

I did receive the scholarship, but I had six months to kill before traveling to Sweden. So I pitched in with housework, helped my little brother, Bobby, study Shakespeare, and tried to keep up my Swedish. I only wished I had a conversation partner, but there were no Swedes or Swedish speakers about. Or so I thought…

One August afternoon, my father came home from work with extraordinary news. A man he'd met through business had a twenty-something son who not only spoke Swedish but lived close by.

It was clear the two fathers wanted to set us up, because my dad thrust the son's phone number into my hand without ceremony. I wasn't opposed to the idea, especially when I learned that the guy—whom I'll call Hans—planned to travel to Sweden the following May, at which time I'd still be there.

I phoned him that evening, and we had so much in common, we chatted for over an hour. Several long phone calls later, I invited him to spend the weekend with my family. I say family, but since my older brother lived in Tampa and my parents were in Germany for Oktoberfest, Bobby and I were alone in the house.

My lengthy conversations with Hans had convinced me I knew him pretty well. Still, I waited with bated breath for his arrival. When his knock sounded on the door, I must've jumped a foot off the couch. Hand on heart, I hurried to the foyer and paused to take a deep breath. Then I opened the door.

Ice blue eyes met my gaze and seemed to pierce my soul. For the next few seconds, a turbulent stream of thought and feeling coursed through me.

No, not him. How did he find me? I can't let him in… not into this house, not into my life.

It may sound silly, but I wanted to slam the door in his face. A fraction of a second later, reason and my Southern upbringing—which lauds hospitality above all else—intervened. I could no more be rude than I could explain my misgivings.

Fatefully, I ignored my first impression and opened the door wide. He crossed the threshold, and due to his charm and physical resemblance to Brad Pitt, my defenses crumbled within the hour. By the end of that weekend, our relationship was in full swing, and he'd arranged for me to meet his family.

He left on Sunday, but by Monday night, my mind was occupied with more than our next date. My parents were still in Munich, so Bobby and I were on our own. For the next five nights, in the wee hours of the morning, we awoke simultaneously. His bedroom was across the hall from mine, and we slept with our doors open, which made conversation easy. On those five occasions, our exchange was all but identical.

Bobby: "Jude, are you awake?"
Me: "Yeah, I guess you are too."
Him: "I feel like something's watching me."
Me: "So do I."

The presence seemed almost tangible. Its energy was familiar, and not unlike my new boyfriend's. Nevertheless, it didn't feel friendly.

In retrospect, I think the presence was Hans. I doubt he was consciously aware of his nocturnal visits. But his soul and mine knew that our paths—and our pasts—were intimately connected.

Christmas came, and I celebrated it with Hans's family and with my own. Then I flew to Stockholm for *nyårsafton* (New Year's Eve) and traveled north to Forsa for the start of the winter term.

In the spring, the *folkhögskola* hosted a performance by a theatrical group, and the most stirring song in the program was called "*Häxor.*" It conjured images of revelry and magic under a full moon and asserted that witches still live today.

I guess we do, I thought. *Double, double, toil and trouble. Memory burn and emotion bubble.*

It bubbled all right, for the subject of witchcraft surfaced again and again in the cauldron of my experience. If it hadn't seemed so serious, I might've laughed.

On April 30, I turned twenty-five. On that same date, Sweden celebrates *Valborgsafton.* It's a major holiday with parties galore. Bonfires abound, and little girls dress as witches. How appropriate!

But the only celebration on my mind occurred a few weeks later when I met up with Hans in Stockholm. The first week of our reunion was blissful. After that, our relationship unraveled. The details are irrelevant, except for one event, forever imprinted on my memory.

We had spent the day exploring the diverse shops of *Gamla Stan* (Old Town), but as the afternoon waned, we branched out and discovered a store that offered psychic readings. Hans held back, examining the trinkets on sale at the front of the shop, but I plunged in and requested a reading.

For a good ten minutes, the medium employed the Tarot and answered my questions as best she could. Then she asked if she could hold my hands. Her fingers felt hot, but when her gaze met mine a moment later, its intensity was even hotter.

"Your energy is great," she said, "but something around you is not."

A sequence of emotions rippled across her face, one by one: confusion, shock, alarm, and then resolve. She glanced at Hans, then focused again on me.

"He's not with you, is he?" she whispered.

Without turning, I sensed he'd moved a few steps closer. "*Ja,*" I answered.

The psychic squirmed in her chair, then squeezed my hands. "Listen to me," she urged. "Someone is trying to control you. He did it in a previous life, and now he wants to do it again."

An image from my dreams flashed before me: the seventeenth-century man in black, arrogant and imperious, pointing his finger at me. So clear was the vision that for an instant, it blocked out the medium's face. When it dissolved, her features appeared even more strained.

"Do you understand?" she asked, stressing every syllable.

"Yes," I said with a nod. "I think I do."

The next day, Hans made a move that, in light of the psychic's revelation, was almost predictable. It was a verbal attack, but the pain it caused was so severe, it could've been a knife to my gut. His weapon of choice? False accusation.

Clearly, our association had soured. In fact, it had shriveled to nothing but a dried-up prune. And I had always hated prunes.

Somehow, in the short time since our reunion, I'd lost myself. I became so concerned with his opinions and feelings, they overshadowed my own. I needed to get away...to think, to breathe. So I struck a blow for freedom and stuffed my duffle bag with essentials. After an awkward farewell, I hightailed it to Arlanda Airport and hopped aboard the first available flight to England.

A month later, I returned to Sweden. Hans greeted my return with a perfunctory hug and a request that I move out of the Stockholm apartment. The situation ran parallel to its seventeenth-century counterpart. Only this time, I was cast out of his life, as opposed to a whole village. And since torture and death weren't involved, our souls had made progress.

In hindsight, his decision was best for us both. And who knows? Some part of him might've recognized me from our previous life together. Perhaps the mirror I held up to his soul cast a reflection too dark and distressing to handle. I flew home to Florida and never saw him again. Years later, I learned the full meaning of my dream and the reason for my bizarre reaction when I first met him: in one of his past lives, Hans was the Witchfinder General, Matthew Hopkins, and I was one of many he accused.

INTUITIVE IMPRESSIONS

Intuitive impressions may not be as strong as attraction or repulsion, but they can still provide important clues to past lives. They involve feelings you get about people—and feelings they get about you—that aren't easily dismissed.

Your Impressions of Others

Pay close attention to your impressions of others. An image or words might pop into your head at first glance, upon meeting them, after a short acquaintance, or even after a long one.

Just before our sons started preschool, Dan and I attended the school's open house. The instant we met the head teacher, Ms. C., the three of us felt a deep connection. She even gave us her phone number—which she admitted she never did with someone she'd just met—and suggested her two daughters as potential babysitters for the boys.

As we turned to leave, an odd thought popped into my head.

Tudor England. The royal court.

I said nothing about my impression to Ms. C. Nevertheless, shortly after that first meeting, she became obsessed with Tudor England, particularly Henry VIII and his wives. Her daughters, who became the boys' most beloved babysitters, were also fascinated by the period.

Remember, they moved to town around the same time we did. I couldn't shake the feeling that our families were interlinked, that we'd all been friends and family in several lives. For no reason I could articulate, I looked up to Ms. C, and she loved my boys as though they were her own.

Two years later, right after Kim O'Neill told me I'd been Katherine Howard, another insight grabbed hold of me. During that lifetime, Ms. C was Katherine's first cousin and Henry VIII's second wife, Anne Boleyn. Suddenly, Ms. C's predilection for manicures and pride in her near perfect fingernails made a lot of sense; Anne Boleyn was reported to have had "some little show of a nail"—which one sixteenth-century writer exaggerated into a sixth finger—on the side of one of her regular finger-nails.

Both Queen Anne and Queen Katherine were beheaded by order of the king. All things considered, it made sense that Anne and Katherine would enter a subsequent lifetime with neck issues. Luckily, mine have been resolved, and my neck is solid as a rock these days. What of Connor's instinct about our necks? Funny that he, too, hurt his neck when Ms. C and I were on hand to comfort him.

When I told Ms. C of my impressions, she accepted them without hesitation. She already felt a strong connection to Anne Boleyn and was positive that Connor had played a role during that lifetime. I asked her who she thought Connor had been, and with a literal shiver of recognition, she confirmed what I already suspected.

For validation, I contacted a local channeler, who confirmed that I was Katherine Howard and Ms. C was indeed Anne Boleyn. He revealed that Connor did play an important role in that life, but for personal reasons I hope you'll respect, I don't want to give his identity. The channeler also said that my friend Sylvia's brother, José, was an ambassador to France in that lifetime. Thomas Boleyn—Anne's father and Katherine's uncle—actually served in that capacity for a time, and I felt certain that José was Thomas Boleyn.

Ms. C and her daughters were also involved in the seventeenth-century life in England, during which Matthew Hopkins terrorized countless women with his accusations. In addition to the lower-back torture, many women were subjected to a public spectacle called "swimming." It was essentially a trial by water, during which the accused was bound and thrown into a river or lake. If they floated—which sup-posedly proved that God's holy water rejected them—they were guilty; if they sank, they were innocent.

After I realized that my ex-boyfriend Hans had been Hopkins, I felt compelled to talk with Ms. C. Without reveal-ing my suspicions, I posed a few questions. Her answers were telling.

Like me, she suffered from low back pain and had a thing about false accusation. She didn't swim and was terrified of her children drowning. Both of her daughters experienced in-tense ear pain if they went under water. All three of them felt drawn to English history, and the older daughter had been fascinated by the subject of medieval midwives since middle school.

Bingo. Once again, my intuitive impressions gave me the initial clues to a past-life connection.

Others' Impressions of You

If a person you've just met senses that you're somehow con-nected to a place, a profession, or to him/her, don't dismiss it out of hand. Consider the impression and see if it resonates with you. If it does, you've likely stumbled onto another clue.

The morning after my dream of seventeenth-century England and my viperous accuser, I started classes at UW-Madison. Swedish was first on the agenda, and the teacher was so young and approachable that I strode to his office right after class.

I guess he didn't hear my entrance, because when I ven-tured a "hello," he jumped at his desk. Then he swiveled around to face me.

After a few preliminaries, I asked, "What's the Swedish word for witch?"

Instantly, his expression changed. He looked half bewildered, half amused. "It's odd you should ask that," he said, "and I hope you won't take this the wrong way, but I wouldn't be surprised if you were one."

"A witch?"

"Yes. Are you?"

I let out a strangled laugh. "Not this time around."

He gave me a searching look, then nodded. "I understand," he said. "I thought you had that vibe about you. I dated one once. The word you want is *häxa*. *Häxor* is the plural."

I repeated the new words and thanked him for his honesty as much as the information. His impression, right on the heels of my dream, gave me plenty to ponder.

Three years later, when I flew to England to escape my Swedish ex-boyfriend, I traveled to Boscastle, a coastal village in a picturesque valley with an inlet that snakes out to the sea. I explored the harbor's sixteenth-century quay and visited the Museum of Witchcraft.

A couple days later, I traveled to the village of Witheridge and met the man who founded the museum, Cecil Williamson. He'd also established a witchcraft museum on the Isle of Man, and during World War II, he founded the Witchcraft Research Centre, which gathered information about Nazi occultism for British intelligence and facilitated the capture of Rudolf Hess.

Mr. Williamson was an extraordinary individual, both historian and wise man. I guess he sensed my sincerity and perhaps my past-life associations with witchcraft, because he invited me to his home and spoke at length and with great candor about his beliefs and remarkable life. I returned the favor by relating some of my experiences to him. He sensed that I'd been a witch in other lives and thought I might resume the practice in this one.

I'll never forget his parting words: "If you should choose the way of the witch, get to know your shadow. That's the best advice anyone can give."

Later, alone in bed, I mulled over his words. Everyone possesses light and shadow within. In order to choose the one, we have to confront the other. We shouldn't focus on negativity, but denying it only gives it power; staring it straight in the face, armed with the light of unconditional love, is the key to change. Self-knowledge creates awareness, which, in turn, allows us to transcend the ego's hold and seek enlightenment. Then we can truly become a force for good.

I wasn't a witch—not in this life, at least—but I was learning the shadow side of both my personality and the chief archetypes influencing it. Moreover, I'd discovered shades of my soul through glimpses of past lives and insights into their connections with my present.

Some impressions inspire not just greater understanding, but healing as well. During my ten-month period of chronic pain in Williamsburg, I repeatedly met with a Reiki master named Alexandra for pain management. She knew nothing of my past, but after our second session together, she gave me a little smile.

"I don't know if this will mean anything," she began, "but while I was working on you, I got a clear impression of a Viking ship with a close-up view of the carved bow. It was from one of your earlier lives, and I could see you staring out to sea, with the wind blowing your long, blond hair. You were some kind of pagan priestess in the Norse tradition, and you were extremely powerful. Actually, it feels like your healing in the present is about you reclaiming your power."

Her impressions meant more than she could guess, for they matched up with a ninth-century past life I'd already uncovered. In that life, I was a Norse seer and priestess named Ota, and I was married to a Viking named Thorgestr who invaded Ireland and declared himself King of Dublin.

Alexandra wasn't finished. "Two other things came to the surface," she said. "They could be children, but whatever they are, they're happy to finally be expressed."

All at once, I knew she was right. My physical plight was bringing up all kinds of baggage from my past—however far back it stretched—so it could now be healed. I had no doubt I'd loved and lost two young boys in the past, one of them from drowning.

Don't ask me how I knew it, but the accompanying sorrow was so intense that as soon as I got home, I wrote a poem in the children's memory. It was a long one, but my pen flew across the page without pause, and I completed it in just ten minutes. I read it to Dan and cried a few tears. Then I threw it away and felt lighter in spirit than I had in months.

Years later in Florida, when my sons were two years old, our family had a serious case of the bath-time blues. Geoffrey was deathly afraid of baths, and once he panicked, Connor invariably chimed in. I couldn't help but wonder if Geoffrey had drowned in a past life. My practical side questioned it. My intuition hinted that Geoffrey had been the child I lost to drowning in a time long past.

I'd recently met a BodyTalk practitioner named Lisa. As it turned out, she was also a massage therapist and intuitive and made house calls to boot. On one visit, she worked one-on-one with the boys. Afterward—without any knowledge of my suspicions about Geoffrey's past—she confirmed them.

"Geoffrey's fear of the bath comes from drowning in a past life," she said.

The final confirmation came in the form of a dream, about a month before the boys' fifth birthday. Geoffrey and I were standing on a dock, and I had the distinct impression we were in Ireland. As I stared out at the rippling water, Geoffrey pulled away from me and jumped into it. He disappeared beneath the surface, and panic paralyzed me. A moment later, I leapt feet-first into the water and sank down, down... deeper than I anticipated. By the time my feet touched his body, it was perfectly still. I was too late. He was dead.

Grief wrenched me from the dream, and I ran to the boys' bedroom to make sure both of them were still breathing. After four decades of dreams about drowning boys, I realized that Ireland was the setting for the tragedy and that Geoffrey (in that other life) was around five years old when it happened. I prayed with my whole being that he and Connor would stay safe in this life. Wouldn't you know, a year later, Geoffrey nearly drowned during his first swimming lesson. Thankfully, he lived to tell the tale.

The Viking woman, Ota, was thought to have had sons, but there's no mention of one drowning. Since the bulk of history remains a mystery, I have to trust my instincts and the intuitive impressions of others.

When exploring past lives, relationships are key. Individuals who attract or repel you right from the start might be people you've known in other lives. First impressions, whether yours or someone else's, can help you fill in the blanks and reinforce your findings.

6

SPONTANEOUS SHIFTS IN CONSCIOUSNESS OR TIME

Have you ever woken from a dream and known it was real? Have you suspected that time travel was possible without the bells and whistles of a futuristic machine? If so, this chapter is right up your alley. If not, it's time to consider the shifts in consciousness and time that can and do occur.

DREAMS

When you dream, you access the subconscious, which holds all memory through time and space. So the images and symbols that crop up in dreams can be or represent past-life memories. That's why it's important to keep a dream journal, or at least to leave paper and pen beside your bed. That way, you can write down the events and details from your dreams before you forget them.

Of course, some dreams are so vivid, you never forget them. I had such a dream during my senior year of college.

My wrists burned as I struggled to free my hands from the rope that bound them behind my back. The cart jostled along a dirt road, conveying me to a destination I neither desired nor deserved. In front of me, the man on horseback stared dead ahead; I sensed he wanted to sneak a peek over his shoulder but didn't dare. Other men strode alongside the cart, murmuring to each other in English and French, but they also avoided my gaze.

I looked up. The restless sky became an eddy of swirling clouds, gray ghosts who spied on the scene unfolding below. To my right, a clearing extended down the hill toward a lake. To my left, an army of towering trees stretched their great arms over the road in a canopy of rustling leaves. It seemed a benediction, not for the oblivious men, but for me and the friend who sat bound in a second cart behind me.

I twisted around and responded to her anxious stare with a silent message I knew she'd intuit: Mind your fears. Be calm. Remember, this is all illusion. They can do nothing in truth to harm us.

She nodded. Then her gaze fixed on the tear in her long, brown skirt. A moment later, she began to laugh.

The men on foot flinched. A few crossed themselves while those on horseback reined in their mounts. Others rushed toward her, eager to quash her outburst.

I awoke with a shock. Was the woman all right? How had the men silenced her? Had I fared any better?

I shook my head to clear it.

It was just a dream, I told myself, but somehow the words rang false. I knew in my gut it stemmed from a past life. It wasn't the first such dream, and it wouldn't be the last. Connecting those dreams to other lives helped me understand why they were so potent.

Your intention to learn about past lives will open the door to achieving that goal. Dreams offer a nightly opportunity to gather information, so seize it. Just before you go to sleep, state your intention either mentally or aloud. You can also pray to receive information and ask to retain clear memories upon waking. When you wake, write down everything you remember. Even the smallest clue can be specific enough to aid your research.

One morning when Connor was six, he approached me while I was cooking breakfast. "Mommy, I want to talk about another life," he said. "I was a Viking. You were a Viking too, but you were a lady."

I flipped a pancake and asked him to tell me more. He said it was a long time ago and I'd find out more later. Then he ran off to play with Geoffrey.

My intuition told me he'd referred to my life as the Norse seer/priestess/queen, Ota, and I wanted to ensure that his prediction (about learning more later) came true. So that night, as I lay down to sleep, I set my intention.

I really want to learn more about my life as Ota, I prayed.

Shortly after, I fell asleep and dreamed of Sylvia's brother, José, for the first time in more than a decade.

We were standing—possibly floating—in a courtyard surrounded by whitewashed buildings with parapets and arches of Moorish design. He wore a flowing robe and spoke in a language I could barely make out. All at once, I understood.

Why is he speaking Arabic? I wondered. *This meeting is connected to Ota, so Irish or Old Norse would make more sense. Why Arabic?*

Then Dan was at my side. I didn't see him, but felt him; his "energy signature" was as clear to me as my own. Sticking close to a pillared walkway, the three of us moved through the courtyard in contented silence.

The next morning, I did more research on Thorgestr and Ota and came across information I'd missed before. An ambassador from Cordova (in Muslim Spain) traveled to the Viking court in Ireland, and he and Ota became friends almost at once. She apparently gave him many gifts, and he regaled her with stories of his home country and Muslim history.

The Moorish ambassador's name was a mouthful—Yahya bn-Hakam el Bekri al Djayani—but he was known as *al-Ghazal* ("the Giselle"). The nickname struck a chord deep inside me, and I recalled the first time José held my hand and my impression that we'd shared a life that was somehow connected with Spain. I couldn't escape the conclusion that José was al-Ghazal in a previous life.

Not long afterward, I spoke with an experienced channeler and asked him to focus in on the Viking age in Ireland to determine both my past-life identity and José's. He connected me with Ota and José with al-Ghazal.

My dream set the stage for this validation. Just by clueing me in on Arabic, it guided my research and provided a breakthrough.

If a recurring dream focuses on a specific location or a time period before you were born, pay special attention to it. Write down every detail you can remember about the location, the people, and what you were thinking while the dream was in progress. Someday, you might find yourself in that same location and get the chance to solve the mystery. I was fortunate to get such a chance after repeatedly reliving the following dream:

> *I floated down a long, narrow room that seemed a glorified hallway toward a forbidden door. It was part of a sumptuous residence... a house, but not a home.*
>
> They know, *I thought as the door swam closer.* They'll be here any second.
>
> *Footsteps on the stairs. Shadows on the wall. The closed door was but an arm's length away.*
>
> The king, *I thought.* He's in there.
>
> *A blood red curtain appeared in front of the door, barring me from the room and the man on the other side. I floated backward, lost and alone.*

This dream cropped up again and again during my last two years of high school. I couldn't comprehend its meaning or its persistence; I only knew it had something to do with England, a country I hoped to visit one day.

Then, in the summer of 1987, I traveled there with my parents. During the brief trip, two historic sights resonated with me on a visceral level: Hever Castle and Hampton Court Palace. In the sixteenth century, Hever was Anne Boleyn's home, and although I couldn't fathom why, I felt an immediate connection to it. From the moment we entered the courtyard, a strangely familiar blend of desire and respect rose within me, and it was linked to an energy that seemed a part of the walls themselves.

"I could live here," my mother said as we toured the home.

"So could I," I replied. Inside, I wondered if she actually had lived there, as a long-forgotten guest.

Hampton Court was a different matter. The façade was striking and stately, but a peculiar sense of unease came over me as we approached the entrance. I said nothing about it to my parents, but the feeling kept pace with our progress right up until the moment when the tour guide led us to the Long Gallery.

I know this place, I thought.

It was the "hallway" from my dreams. According to the guide, it led to the Chapel Royal, which was closed to visitors that day.

So that's what's on the other side of the door, I thought. *A chapel.*

My entrance had been blocked so many times in my dreams; now it was the same story in real life. For some reason, the irony of the situation struck me as funny, and at that point, my disquiet dissolved. I figured my dreams had been some form of precognition and left it at that.

Years later, after learning I was Katherine Howard, research helped to explain my recurring dream. After Katherine was accused of adultery at Hampton Court Palace, she broke from her guards and ran along the gallery toward the chapel, where the king was at prayer. She hammered on the door and cried out to her husband, begging an audience with him, but the guards seized her and dragged her back down the gallery to her own rooms.

Most historians believe she was seventeen or eighteen years old when she died. Maybe that's why my dream about the forbidden door began when I was seventeen and persisted into my eighteenth year.

Ever since her death on February 13, 1542, people have reported seeing a woman in white floating down the gallery toward the chapel. She's believed to be the ghost of Katherine Howard.

I think of my recurring dream, and I have to question whether it was really a dream or an astral trip. Is a part of my past—or my energy—locked in a residual haunting at Hampton Court? When people catch a glimpse of Katherine's ghost, are they actually seeing me?

ASTRAL TRIPS

Astral projection—also known as the out-of-body experience—is the natural ability of the spirit to leave the physical body. Astral travel is basically the same as astral projection, except that you experience both the journey and the destination. Believe it or not, your spirit often leaves your body during sleep, so some of your "dreams" are actually astral trips. They happen spontaneously and sometimes take you into past lives.

How can you tell the difference between an astral trip and a dream? Astral travel includes the following: (1) a clear, rational sequence of events; (2) observing yourself from the outside, i.e., moving into and/or out of your body; and (3) the sensation of floating or flight under your own power.

Your travel speed will determine whether or not you "fly" during your experience. In general, spirits use three different speeds: a slow pace comparable to a stroll; an intermediate rate characterized by the sensation of a rushing, roaring wind; or the speed of thought, which instantly brings a spirit to its destination. If, while "dreaming," you suddenly find yourself in a distant land and/or an earlier time in history, your spirit used the speed of thought to get there.

Some people practice astral projection with intent and on a regular basis, but my experience with astral travel has been more spontaneous. It happens when it happens, and I hold on to my awareness when it does. The best advice I can give you is to pay attention to your dreams—and astral trips disguised as dreams—while they're occurring and after you wake.

If, during a "dream," you find yourself moving into someone you've observed from the outside—or moving out of the body you just inhabited—that body/personality is, in most cases, one of your past-life identities. In my experience, when I'm inside another body, I merge completely with the personality inside it. The moment my mind switches to observation mode (third-person analysis), I shift back out again.

When I was thirty-one, shortly after I moved into Dan's Williamsburg apartment, I had a dream I'm certain was an astral trip. I drifted with the wind over fjord and field to what seemed a farewell scene. A woman with long, tangled hair stood beside a horse and rider. The man astride the horse had shoulder-length, red hair and a full beard, and I sensed he was a prominent person.

I floated toward the young woman's back and then became her. The mergence held long enough for me to exchange good-byes with the man. Then I shifted back out of her and hovered in the air, regaining my modern identity.

Suddenly, as if I'd been whacked over the head with Thor's hammer, information flooded my mind. It was the tenth century, and we'd spoken Old Norse. The red-haired man had attended an important meeting and was setting out on a long journey. I (as the woman) had used precognitive skills to verify his safety and success. I knew he cared for me and hoped we'd be reunited soon. Less clear was our exact location. I received a strong impression of Iceland, but murmurs beyond it hinted at the Hebrides and a land of promise far to the west.

Then it dawned on me: the character on horseback was Dan. The one looked nothing like the other, but their essence was the same. This was no dream; it was a moment in history, from Dan's past and mine. I experienced it as both the observer and the observed.

Spontaneous Slips

Whether or not you explore past lives, you could experience spontaneous slips in time or personality while you're awake. You literally shift into another time or personality, or it shifts into you. The underlying fact that all time is "now" makes this phenomenon possible.

These slips usually occur without warning, and the trigger could be anything. It could be a person you've known in another life or who embodies the archetype of someone you once knew. It could be a past-life artifact, anything that reminds your soul of the object, or something that symbolizes it; e.g., a movie from the appropriate time period, a piece of jewelry, an article of clothing, a landscape, a building, etc.

Strong emotion can trigger slips as well. For example, joy, rage, or sorrow over a present situation punches a hole through the illusion of time and space and lets in—just for a moment—a snapshot of a past life during which you experienced that same emotion. If it happens, don't brush it off as "one of those things." Stay aware and consider the possibility that you're connecting with another part of your soul.

Time Slips

In my experience, spontaneous slips in time are triggered most often by a specific place, especially a location you visited in another life or one that reminds you of a past-life location. As I once found out, it can also be a place your past-life self never visited but where those who inhabited the space felt a connection to you or spoke of you.

During my 1993 trip to England, I stopped in Winchester for a couple of hours and decided to check out the cathedral. The first church was built there in 648, but the present building—originally a Benedictine monastery—was begun in 1079.

Some of the Norman architecture remained, but as I explored the nave, a recurrent thought filled my mind: *Older…I need to go older.*

Bonkers, right? But it gets better. I started to feel like I was being watched, maybe even followed. I glanced around at the potpourri of international tourists, but they all ignored me, just as they should.

The whisper of a foreign tongue slithered in and out of the stone arches. It seemed Germanic, so I guessed it was Old English. Before long, a tingling sensation tickled my ears.

An old expression leapt to mind … that your ears burn when someone speaks of you.

At the time, I entertained the possibility that a ghost was trying to communicate with me. Later, I learned that the tenth-century Bishop Aethelwold of Winchester made Aethelthryth—the seventh-century abbess who was one of my past-life personalities—a major role model during his Benedictine reform. I must've tapped into a moment in time when he or someone else was talking about me, i.e., the "me" I used to be. It could have been the very echo that tickled my ears.

Personality Slips

Slips in personality are usually brief. While in progress, the thoughts and opinions of the other personality seem quite natural until, a few seconds later, your current self chimes in and you start to analyze what just happened. I experienced such a slip—involving two of my past-life identities—one night a few years ago while watching TV.

The 2007 motion-capture film *Beowulf* filled the screen. I hadn't seen the movie when it was first released, but now I was riveted. The moment the blond queen, Wealthow, came on screen, I slipped into a kind of trance.

I felt a strong responsibility to my king, my family, and those in my care. I longed to commune with the gods. I also experienced an incongruous desire for period jewelry, especially necklaces. The part of me that was a ninth-century, blond Viking queen had resonated with the on-screen image and surfaced.

Suddenly, a belief in one God and a passionate sense of duty toward humanity as a whole emerged. Guilt over the desire for jewelry flooded me. These feelings sprang from the mind and heart of Aethelthryth. As a matter of fact, in her later years she developed a painful swelling under her jaw that she believed was punishment for wearing jewelry—particularly necklaces—in her youth.

All at once, the love of jewelry returned, together with a thirst for adventure and the unmistakable call of the sea. Strangest of all, when King Hrothgar (played by Anthony Hopkins) spoke the queen's name, I didn't hear the word "Wealthow." I heard the name of my ninth-century past-life personality, Ota. The realization snapped me out of my trance, and I was my modern self again.

To understand how bizarre some of my impressions were, you must know one thing: I couldn't care less about jewelry in this lifetime. The desire and guilt my past-life selves experienced don't even compute. Yet during the slip, they did.

As you can see, dreams, astral trips, and spontaneous slips provide valuable information about past lives. If you remain open to experience and cultivate your awareness, further clues will emerge.

7

WHEN THE PAST POPS UP
IN THE PRESENT

We've already discussed spontaneous slips, but the phenomena in this chapter are different because in most cases, you're fully conscious in the present moment when they occur. Your past-life experience simply pops up to say hello. It can manifest as déjà vu, inexplicable abilities, and unexpected behavior. It also finds an outlet in the many forms of creative expression. We'll look at each phenomenon, one at a time.

DÉJÀ VU

Déjà vu is the feeling of having experienced something before, even when it's your first time experiencing it, and it's a common phenomenon. Sometimes that feeling is actually a split-second memory of charting a specific experience for your current incarnation on the Other Side prior to your birth. As Sylvia Browne explains in her book *Phenomenon*, you include both important and trivial details in your pre-incarnation chart for every lifetime, and as those details occur on Earth, your spirit can resonate so strongly with them—and with the memory of choosing them—that it reverberates through your subconscious and conscious mind. This type of déjà vu can reassure you that you're aligned with your chart and what you came here to do.

Other times, déjà vu is about past-life memories. Something seems familiar to you because it is familiar. I experienced this form of déjà vu during my first date with my husband, Dan.

Our dinner was a long one, so long that we were the last customers to leave the restaurant. Nonetheless, we were reluctant to part, so we went to Dan's apartment to watch a movie.

I should've been nervous for two reasons: (1) he invited me to his apartment on the first date, and (2) the video we viewed was *Silence of the Lambs*. Yet my only real concern was my new job, which would begin the next morning. Sitting beside Dan on the couch, I turned to him and confessed my worries.

He covered my hand with his. "You'll do fine," he said.

Serenity, surrender, and a strong sense of déjà vu rushed through me. I believed him. I also believed we'd sat beside each other in just that way hundreds of times before. This wasn't our first shared journey, and it might not be our last.

This man will support me, I thought. *He will protect me with his life.*

From then on, we spent all of our free time together. But despite our instant familiarity, we were still surprised when we learned each other's ages. I assumed he was older than me, and he thought I was younger; actually, the reverse was true. Our assumptions had nothing to do with our appearance, and the déjà vu I experienced was no accident. Both stemmed from unconscious memories of a previous life together in fifteenth-century Ireland.

INEXPLICABLE ABILITIES

If you've already examined your childhood, you may have uncovered such clues, but inexplicable abilities can surface at any age in dreams, astral trips, and the waking world. You might speak a foreign language, show a talent, or use a skill you never learned in this life. You might just know about a subject you never studied; it could be a case of claircognizance, but it could also be past-life knowledge rising to the surface.

When I was twenty-five, I traveled to Glastonbury, England. The day I arrived, I met a Swedish woman who was a fellow guest at my bed and breakfast. Besides Sweden, we had our age and our interests in common, and she introduced me to a thirty-something Swedish man and his young son. She'd only just met them, as I'd just met her, but the four of us felt an instant connection.

We spent the day together touring the sites. On the grounds of Glastonbury Abbey, we encountered a clairvoyant who told us point blank we'd been companions in a past life, long before the abbey was ever built. Apparently, she'd observed us from a distance and received a psychic flash she felt compelled to share. Her revelation surprised no one, but it was a welcome validation that our instincts were right on target.

That evening, we wound up in a pub, where we chatted with a friendly group of locals. We discussed diverse topics, and soon the talk turned to two ancient oaks near Glastonbury Tor: the Gog and the Magog. The trees were supposedly part of an earlier Druidic grove, and one of them was sick. The locals invited us to join them on a late-night visit to the site so that, together, we could infuse the tree with healing energy.

An intense feeling of déjà vu hit me as we approached the great oaks. Either I'd been to that spot before or I'd venerated other oaks through sacred rituals long ago.

We surrounded the ailing tree and clasped hands. A woman led us in prayer, then spoke an incantation as we circled the tree. We stopped, laid our hands on the tree, and closed our eyes.

My chest swelled with sudden love for nature in general and the tree in particular. Then a powerful force entered the top of my head and rushed into my heart. I sent the energy down the length of my arms, into my hands, and, finally, into the tree. It flowed for several minutes until I sensed the infusion was complete. Then I opened my eyes and removed my hands, and my companions did the same. We stepped away in unison.

The woman who'd spoken and one of the men seemed familiar with the healing ceremony, but the rest of us acted on instinct. We'd simply known what to do, and I couldn't help but wonder if skills we'd learned in past lives played a role in our present.

Here's another example, involving an inexplicable ability during sleep and what I learned about it. During my first autumn in Salem, Massachusetts, I had a vivid dream I believe was an astral trip. I was inside a cottage in the woods, and I sat at a wooden table across from an older woman with unkempt, gray hair. She was my friend and my teacher; the subject at hand was magic. After a point, I "separated" from myself and analyzed the scene from the viewpoint of my present life.

We're speaking Welsh, I thought. It was a language I hadn't learned in this life.

Then I was sucked back into consciousness. I rolled over in bed, comforted by the memory and the older woman within it.

A murmur had followed me from the depths of the dream into my present reality. It sounded like either *Gwenllian* or *Gwendolyn.* I seized the more familiar name and smiled.

"Gwendolyn," I said aloud. A blast from the past for sure.

I'd always wanted to travel to Wales. Thanks to an inexplicable desire to learn Welsh, I nearly studied there—instead of Scotland—for my junior year abroad. If my dream was any indication, I already knew the language and had spoken it long ago.

Four years later, I traveled to Wales with my parents. We spent a day in Conwy, a walled, medieval town on the north coast of Wales, and I immediately sensed a connection. That night, while my father and I slept, my mother heard me speaking Welsh. When she told me the next morning, I wasn't surprised, for I'd spoken the language with Gwendolyn in my dreams. Being on Welsh soil must've triggered my memory. Either that or a part of me actually conversed with my spirit guide while the other part slept.

A decade later, I broached the subject of past lives with the same psychic team mentioned in previous chapters. They said I'd lived in Wales more than once, and during at least one lifetime there, I'd done white magic in the Celtic tradition.

I asked them to channel information specific to the name "Gwendolyn." They said that she and I had worked magic together in a cottage but were caught and confined in a brick building. I apparently knew her in several lifetimes, and she'd been one of my spirit guides from the moment I was born into this life.

That revelation stirred the memory of my first childhood doll. I named her Edyann. When viewed from a linguistic perspective—or from that of a mother whose toddlers passed over sounds they couldn't pronounce —"Edyann" was probably Gwendolyn.

Both the doll and the woman had tousled hair. Edyann's, however, had the added distinction of looking spiked, since I carried her around by the hair. Did Gwendolyn have matted hair in my "dream" because my subconscious linked her with the doll? Or did I muss the doll's hair in the first place because I remembered my guide's dishevelment in a life long past?

I decided to do some research, but where to start? Regarding Wales, the two most significant events of my life related to a woman called Gwenllian or Gwendolyn and St. David's Cathedral, which was built on the site of a sixth-century monastery founded by the country's patron saint, David. Intuition drove me to seek out any connection between the two.

St. David was supposed to have been born during a violent storm, and his mother was St. Non. Her sister (David's aunt) was St. Gwen. There was a reference to "Gwendolyn, Abbess in Wales" whose feast day was October 31, but I found no further information to corroborate it.

David's early childhood was spent at his mother's convent, Ty Gwyn, near Whitesand Bay. He was also connected to Glastonbury, where he reputedly built a church near the old one.

I recalled the three Swedes I'd met in Glastonbury. When we'd toured the abbey grounds, the clairvoyant we'd met had said we'd known one another in a time before the abbey was built. Was it during David's time? Had we known him or any of his family?

Then I spotted an article on the first woman in Wales to be hanged for witchcraft. She was a weaver, healer, and wise woman in the late sixteenth century, and her name was Gwen *ferch* (daughter of) Ellis. Apparently, people came from far and wide to seek not only her advice, but healings, for themselves and their animals. They also sought protection against malevolent neighbors who might take the form of "nightwolves."

Unfortunately, one of her incantations was discovered in Gloddaeth Hall—the home of the powerful Thomas Mostyn, justice of the peace—and she confessed to spending a night there while he was away. Gloddaeth Hall is known today as St. David's College.

Gwen ferch Ellis was flung into Flint Jail in 1594, and seven "witnesses" gave evidence against her during an official investigation in Llansanffraid Glan Conwy. Conwy … the same area that had seemed familiar to me just before I spoke Welsh in my sleep.

Was Gwen ferch Ellis my spirit guide? Had she been St. Gwen in a previous life?

Whatever the case, my inexplicable ability to speak Welsh in Salem and Conwy came from a past life—or lives—in Wales. My spirit guide Gwendolyn played a role in at least one of those lives.

UNEXPECTED BEHAVIOR

Unexpected behavior can be associated with past lives. An emotional outburst with no obvious source could be a past-life memory of which you're not even conscious. You could assume the customs of another culture or tradition, e.g., using a quality or pattern of speech that doesn't exist in your native tongue or knowing instinctively how to behave in a situation you've never encountered in this lifetime. You might also make odd, spontaneous decisions or watch your desires do a 180 without warning.

During my freshman year at FSU, I met a twenty-something English tourist one night in a bar. Within minutes of introducing ourselves, we left our respective friends and the noisy bar and began a dialogue that lasted for hours. He was traveling north in the morning, so by evening's end, we exchanged addresses and promised to write.

Our behavior was odd. Neither of us was in the habit of abandoning our friends, and I left the safety of a crowded bar with a total stranger. What's more, we both felt compelled to keep in touch.

E-mail and the Internet were almost nonexistent then, which made old-fashioned letters the name of the game. Overseas delivery slowed correspondence to a snail's pace, but on average, I received two lengthy letters per month for the next year and a half.

During that time, a friend and I experimented with a Ouija board, and it gave us an unexpected message: I LOVE YOU. I MISS YOU.

"Who do you miss?" I asked, but I should've known.

JUDY. I MISS YOU.

"What's your name?" I questioned.

TOM.

I racked my brains. Tom was a common enough name, but I couldn't match it to any of my friends.

Abruptly, the planchette's rhythm changed. It jerked across the board, then circled with increasing speed.

"Is this still Tom?" I asked.

The planchette whipped to NO. Nevertheless, the spirit's identity seemed connected to Tom, as if it were a long-forgotten part of him, a part that was more intense and sinister.

"Who are you?" I questioned.

The planchette zipped around the board, but its pace prevented an answer.

I looked up at my friend. "Are you moving this thing?"

Fear wavered in her eyes. "No, I thought you were."

The next instant, the planchette slipped from our fingers and tumbled to the floor. We returned it to the board and moved it over GOOD-BYE several times as we said the word aloud. Then I heaved a sigh of relief.

Our experiment yielded more questions than answers, but a week later, I received a letter from the Englishman, who conveyed a surprising tidbit. He'd decided to use his middle name. His friends now called him "Tom," and he invited me to do the same.

During my sophomore year of college, I studied abroad in London. Here, finally, was the opportunity to hook up with Tom in Yorkshire. The reunion was highly anticipated ... by him, by me, and even by my roommates.

You see, I was still a virgin. A weekend alone with an attractive guy offered a host of romantic possibilities; one in particular seemed a foregone conclusion.

But from the moment Tom and I connected at the train station, something was off. His appearance hadn't changed much, and his personality was consistent with his numerous letters. So what was the deal?

Our first night together, we kissed, and his attentions grew heated. I allowed them up to a point, mostly because I was determined to ignore my ridiculous reaction to his presence.

You must understand: I was more than a little curious about sex. Frankly, I was ripe for the picking. In Tallahassee, I had been ready to jump Tom's bones. In his home country, my inner self demanded distance.

This is insane, I thought. *What's wrong with me? I'm going to be an author, and authors need experience!*

Despite that questionable logic, my virtue remained intact the following morning. Tom was in every way a gentleman and not a bad tour guide. We ventured into Cumbria and did a little sightseeing in the Lake District. The brisk wind and ashen sky renewed my spirits. I gazed into the gray waters of Lake Windermere and made a silent promise.

Tonight's the night. Come hell or high water, I'm sleeping with him.

That night, in a cozy cottage, we snuggled in front of the TV. Then the unthinkable happened.

I fell asleep. Not only that, but I slept through the night!

I woke with the dawn and shuffled to the loo. To my surprise, I started my period. It was two weeks early, and it was never early. My cycles were like clockwork … until that weekend.

My plan for physical intimacy had come to a screeching halt, yet an odd mixture of guilt and relief washed over me. I broke the news to my companion, and he took it well. But on the train ride back to London, I wondered if I was destined to remain a virgin forever.

I heard from Tom just once more, ten years after I left him in Yorkshire. He telephoned me out of the blue while I was visiting my parents in Florida. His speech was slurred, but he attributed it to painkillers. Then he blurted out words that took me right back to that strange night with the Ouija board: "I love you! I miss you! Why did I let you get away? I should never have let you go!"

It was an awkward moment, one of many we shared. But I came to understand our relationship years later while reading up on one of my past-life selves, Aethelthryth.

Aethelthryth's ambition was always to be a nun, but she was married off twice before achieving it. Out of either respect or indifference, her first husband, Tondberht, allowed her to remain a virgin. When he died in 655, she retired to the Isle of Ely, which Tondberht had gifted to her. In 660, political considerations forced her to marry Ecgfrith, the second son of Oswiu, King of Northumbria.

Ecgfrith was only fifteen—much younger than Aethelthryth—when she married him, and she convinced him to respect her vow of perpetual virginity. During that time, she apparently visited her friend (some say relative) St. Hilda, abbess of a monastery at Whitby (then known as Streonshalh) in Yorkshire.

Yorkshire … that's where I spent most of my ill-fated weekend with Tom, I thought.

I kept reading. Ecgfrith worshiped Aethelthryth from a distance, but ten years into their marriage—when he ascended to the Northumbrian throne—he wanted her in his bed.

Ten years after our weekend in Yorkshire, Tom phoned me unexpectedly and sounded obsessed. Was that Tom talking to me? Or could it have been Ecgfrith?

Aethelthryth fled to Coldingham, and Ecgfrith followed, intent on bringing her back, by force if necessary. She dodged him again and headed south, but he wasn't far behind.

According to one account, she scrambled onto a rocky headland, and the tide rose to an unusual height around it, making it inaccessible to Ecgfrith's men. They waited for the water to recede, but it remained at high tide for seven days. At last, Ecgfrith realized his wife was protected by a higher power and returned home empty-handed. Aethelthryth arrived safely at Ely, where she established and became abbess of a double monastery in 673.

The tides are controlled by the moon, I thought. *The waters remained high for seven days. The moon … the water … seven days. When I was with Tom, my period arrived early and prevented me from sleeping with him!*

Suddenly, my past-life identity as Katherine Howard popped into my mind. Two other memories came crashing home: (1) the name "Tom" on the Ouija board at FSU, and (2) my bizarre reaction to seeing Tom on English soil. What had made the Englishman decide to use his middle name right when we were corresponding with each other? Was "Tom" his name in another life?

Suddenly, I knew. The two distinct personalities that reached me through the Ouija board were two of his past-life selves: Ecgfrith, who knew Aethelthryth, and Thomas Culpeper, one of the men accused of being Katherine's lover.

Historians disagree about what really happened behind closed doors. If Katherine and Thomas did sleep together, they might've done so because of unfinished business from their past lives as Aethelthryth and Ecgfrith. And the fact that both were executed for their "crime" seems a pretty strong incentive for my soul to think twice before repeating the treasonous act in this life. If they were innocent, Katherine may have spurned Thomas's advances for the same reason I dodged Tom's: an inexplicable sense of her past life as Aethelthryth.

Remember, my desire for intimacy did an about-face the moment we met on English soil; even my body rebelled against it. Furthermore, his decision to use his middle name—which was the name I knew him by in another life—came right on the heels of our meeting. So much of our behavior hinted at two previous lifetimes, and I later confirmed both of them.

CREATIVE EXPRESSION

Past-life experience is sometimes channeled through creative expression. That's because the very act of creation puts you in touch with both your source (God/Universal Intelligence) and your soul. It's especially true when you find yourself "in the zone." Your particular form of creative expression —how you do what you do—is unique to you, and it could be almost anything: writing poems or stories, writing music or lyrics, drawing, painting, sculpting, cooking, baking, singing, dancing, a specific way you care for others, etc. Consider your talents, and look for clues within your personal creations.

At age twenty-six, while living in Salem, Massachusetts, I wrote my first novel. The title, *Where There's Smoke*, referred to the network of clues in everyday life that reveal a deeper truth. In some ways, the book was an attempt to assemble the puzzle pieces of my life and shape them into a picture that was part experience, part imagination. The voice of inspiration spoke loud and clear, and I completed a detailed outline in one sitting.

Basic plot: the protagonist, an American graduate student, discovers she had a past life in Ireland. This has a palpable effect on her and the other principal characters, who were also a part of that lifetime. Together, they unearth secrets that resolve a centuries-old conflict.

The outline called for a seventeenth-century incarnation for each of my three central characters: Nicole, the American grad student; Liam, an Irish novelist; and Göran, a Swedish drifter with an innate aversion to Ireland. I knew instantly who each of them should be in seventeenth-century Ireland: Nicole was Catherine, an Anglo-Irish woman who became versed in the Old Ways; Liam was Richard, a wealthy Englishman who lived on his father's estate in Killarney; and Göran was Edward, Richard's English uncle and chaplain of the estate. Edward, a self-righteous bigot with delusions of grandeur, accused Catherine of witchcraft.

As you might've guessed, Göran bore a resemblance to my Swedish ex-boyfriend, Hans. When I outlined the character of his past-life identity (Edward), I described a childhood incident when Edward drowned a sack of kittens for fun. Today, I believe I subconsciously connected my character's actions with those of Matthew Hopkins, the seventeenth-century Witchfinder General who drowned a number of accused women through the public spectacle of "swimming." The kittens in Edward's childhood were but symbols of countless women who lost their lives.

I also intended a ninth-century incarnation for each of the characters, which I outlined but left unnamed. It seemed important that I find real-life people to plug into that outline, though I couldn't fathom why. I simply trusted I'd find what I sought. Nicole/Catherine should be a Norse priestess who traveled to Ireland. Liam/Richard should be a prominent individual, hopefully a Scandinavian king. Göran/Edward should be a ruthless Viking who tore into Ireland, was jealous of his brother (the aforementioned king), and was married to the priestess.

During research, I came across three ninth-century figures that fit the bill. A Viking named Thorgestr (Thorgisl/ Turgeis) invaded Ireland and declared himself King of Dublin. Some believe he was a Danish prince—others say Norwegian, possibly the brother or close kinsman of the reigning king—and his wife, Ota, was not only a queen, but a priestess he regarded as an oracle.

The correlations were perfect, but they didn't stop there. In 846, the Irish deliberately drowned Thorgestr, by order of Maoil-Seachlainn of Meath. It fit so well. Edward's residual angst over being drowned in a past life (as Thorgestr) resulted in a violent childhood act in which *he* held the position of power, just as the real-life Matthew Hopkins's abuse of power led to the drowning of many accused "witches" in the seventeenth century.

Not only that, but I'd written a modern-day scene in which Nicole's framed photograph of the monastic ruins at Glendalough repulsed Göran. I used Glendalough in the story because I'd actually traveled there, but my first instinct was to make it a picture of Clonmacnoise, one of Ireland's greatest monastic centers of learning and literature. Now my research showed that Clonmacnoise was the site of one of Thorgestr's greatest conquests, and his wife, Ota, purportedly gave prophecies from the high altar.

A sudden memory of my ex-boyfriend Hans sprang forward. When we first met up in Stockholm, he surprised me with a gift: a brooch in the shape of an ancient Celtic symbol.

Was Hans Thorgestr? I wondered. *Was I Ota?*

It would be years before I admitted these truths, as well as Hans's incarnation as Matthew Hopkins. But from then on—

for the purposes of my writing—Thorgestr and Hans were one and the same.

One thing more about that novel: I specifically chose the end of the Tudor period as the setting for one of the past lifetimes and gave my protagonist the name "Catherine" for that incarnation. Historians spell Katherine Howard's name with either a "C" or a "K," but she herself spelled it with the latter. In my first novel, I purposely used a "C" to distance myself from the character. An odd impulse, don't you think? Especially since I had no conscious knowledge that I'd once been Katherine Howard.

I wrote two novels in Virginia: *Flight of the Raven* and *Cry of the Wolf.* I believe that both Aethelthryth and Ota influenced them. The novels interwove Christian and pagan traditions, and Northumbria was the setting for both. Aethelthryth's second husband, Ecgfrith, was a son of Oswiu, King of Northumbria. When I wrote the stories, I didn't even know that a woman named Aethelthryth had existed, yet the heroine of the first story was an Anglo-Saxon noblewoman who was forced to marry for political reasons and who agreed to be a dutiful wife in all ways but one: her husband could never bed her. Aethelthryth had placed that same restriction on Ecgfrith.

In the novels, the Saxon heroine lived in a castle called Ravenwood, and the Saxon hero, Wulfstan (Old English for "wolf stone"), practiced a hybrid of Norse and Anglo-Saxon magic and communicated with ravens and wolves. When I came up with the names and plotted the stories, I had no conscious knowledge that the wolf and raven were sacred to the god Odin—something Ota would've known—or that they had a unique relationship in the natural world. They were simply favorites among my animal totems.

I penned all three of those novels years before I confirmed my past lives as Katherine Howard, Ota, and Aethelthryth. Looking back, I see just how much those lives influenced my writing. It's a good bet your past lives have influenced your outlet for creative expression too.

When déjà vu, inexplicable abilities, and unexpected behavior pop up in your experience, don't dismiss them out of hand. Acknowledge them and see what you can learn. Examine your personal creations, whether they're stories, sketches, or extraordinary recipes you created on instinct. Even the smallest clue can lead to a major discovery, so pay attention!

8

EXTRAORDINARY
EXPERIENCE

M any would consider the experiences we've already covered to be extraordinary, but they occur frequently
and are relatively normal when compared to the phenomena
we'll explore in this chapter. Chances are you'll experience the
following at least once during your present lifetime: appari-
tions/visitations and synchronicity. Let's dive in and discover
how and why they happen.

APPARITIONS/VISITATIONS

Few things scare people more than seeing apparitions, i.e.,
ghosts (earthbound) or spirits (crossed over to the Other
Side) who pop in for a visit. Contrary to popular belief, these

visitations can be positive. Yes, they're unexpected and sometimes confusing, but when they happen, try to remember that you're a spirit too. You just happen to be attached to a body at present.

People you've known in past lives can visit you as spirits. It's extremely rare for a spirit who was once your enemy to visit, and when they do, their purpose could be reconciliation. However, most spirit visitors from past lives were once family or friends. On occasion, these past-life visitors also serve as current spirit guides.

While I was living in Wisconsin, a particular spirit visited me several nights in a row. I knew it was male, and although I couldn't see him, I felt and heard him.

In that twilight zone between dreams and full consciousness, he called out to me. The only trouble was he didn't say "Judy." The word was difficult to make out, but it had at least two syllables and included the "k" sound. My first guess upon waking was "Katherine"—an interesting choice, since that was my name in another life—but I couldn't be sure.

He whispered the word in my left ear. Each time I shot up in bed, he zipped to the far corner of my room and lingered there. I didn't know what sixth sense allowed me to trace the movement, but it was as clear to me as anything I might've seen.

The first night, I needed a few minutes to work up the nerve to approach him. I eyed the "empty" corner, waiting for something to materialize, but once I was an arm's length away, the presence simply dissolved.

By the fourth night, I'd had enough. I leapt from my bed and stomped to the same corner. "Who are you?" I demanded.

"If you're going to wake me up every night, the least you can do is show yourself."

No response was forthcoming, but my guest still remained.

I heaved a pointed sigh. "What do you want?"

Utter silence yet again.

"Fine," I said and turned away.

As I trudged back to my bed, the presence faded behind me. I wasn't aware of any further visits in Madison, but shortly after I moved to Salem, another one yanked me out of a deep sleep.

As I sat up, the energy—which this time hovered at my right side—whisked toward an antique mirror on the opposite wall. The energy felt the same as that of the entity who had popped in on me in Wisconsin.

I held my breath, waiting for him to communicate or at least make a move. Like before, he dissipated without imparting so much as a measly "hello."

Years later in Florida, when I started to research the earthly life of my spirit guide Black Hawk, I learned that his name in Meskwaki-Sauk was *Ma-ka-tai-me-she-kia-kiak*. As I pronounced the last two syllables, an intense feeling of love rushed through me. My whole body tingled with the realization that we had once been family and that he was my nighttime visitor in Wisconsin, Massachusetts, and now Florida. I knew beyond the shadow of a doubt that he'd spoken *his* name, not mine, when he first called to me in Madison. I'd heard the last two syllables of his name—"kia-kiak"—upon waking.

He still visits on occasion. I've felt his energy, and my children have reported seeing a Native American man "standing next to the wolf" (my main animal totem) in our house. It's a comforting reminder that Black Hawk and I will always be connected in spirit.

To me, the most intriguing aspect of apparitions/visitations is that a ghost or spirit visitor can be your own self from another life. Just as you can observe another part of yourself during astral travel, so too can those other selves come to call. Every now and then, if the need or curiosity is great enough, they check on your doings. They might even confront you in order to relay an important message that will help you move forward in your current life. The desire for integration and/or to assist another part of your soul is a powerful force that brooks no limitation.

In the wee hours of March 4, 2008, I had a "dream" that I believe was an astral trip. I was lying on a wooden table in a dimly lit room, and two women were there to help me. I was uber-pregnant and about to give birth. All of a sudden, I left my body and drifted toward the nearest wall to join a crowd of others who were watching what still seemed to be "me" on the table. While in my body, I'd glimpsed only two people in the room; outside it, I got the full picture. I guessed the others were spirits and angels, come to witness the birth and give what comfort they could.

I stared at the dark-haired woman on the table. As the babe in her belly stirred and shifted, she flattened her palms over the movement—as if to draw information from it—and began to prophesy aloud.

I strained to hear her words and could almost make them out. Then, with a rush, I woke to the sound of something altogether different. I slid out of bed, strode to the doorway, and peeked around it toward the computer niche. Our computer and printer were restarting themselves.

The dream and this event are linked, I thought. *Is it a message about the imminent birth of something I'm going to write? Should I write about this dream?*

Despite the warm night, goose bumps overtook me. I rubbed my arms and woke Dan.

He checked the computer and printer, as well as our clocks, and determined that we hadn't lost power. If we had, the computer wouldn't have restarted by itself. On the other hand, if the computer had experienced a software failure and restarted itself, the printer shouldn't have been affected.

"What would make them both turn off and then on again?" he said.

What or who?

I got the distinct feeling someone who knew about my dream was responsible. Now I think it was that other part of myself—the dark-haired woman who was still engaged in a different lifetime—that visited me. Perhaps she wanted me to realize the importance of my dream and write about my experience.

Two years later, right after I finished my research on Thorgunna, Connor—then six years old—tugged on my shirt. "Mommy," he said, "I think you lived in Scotland in another life."

I looked down at him. "Why do you say that?" I asked, but I should've guessed the answer.

"I don't know," he said. "I just do."

Later that same day, as I scanned the news feed on Facebook, the name of a friend's sister stood out to me: Freya.

The word might as well have appeared in giant neon letters, because I couldn't stop staring at it. Finally, I shook my head and went downstairs to find Connor lifting a hefty dictionary onto his lap.

He flipped through it. A minute later, he stopped at a particular page and began to read.

"F-F..." he pronounced. "Fr-Freya. Freya."

I gaped at him. Out of all the words on the page and all the words in the dictionary, he chose that one. And his pronunciation was perfect!

In disbelief, I went to him and glanced at the word to which he was pointing. "That's right," I said. "Good reading, honey."

In something of a daze, I turned toward the stairs. Halfway up, I paused.

The dream of the pregnant, dark-haired woman resurfaced, only this time I was awake. All at once, I was back in that dimly lit room on the wooden table, about to give birth.

Then my consciousness shifted out of the woman. *That was Thorgunna,* I thought. *She was frightened, but she trusted the goddess Freya to see her through the pain and the danger of childbirth.*

The image was overpowering. The vision, the emotion, her faith...all rang clear as a bell and reverberated through my soul. If only for that brief moment, Thorgunna and I were one.

SYNCHRONICITY

Synchronicity is "coincidence," i.e., many incidents happening at or around the same time or place, which seem related. Often, it occurs to help you along your spiritual path and/or serves as a message. But sometimes synchronistic events point toward, or confirm, past-life connections. Let me clarify by sharing two real-life examples.

One night a few years ago, a tall, robed figure—which I perceived as male—spoke to me in a dream.

Another one, he said. *Salisbury. You were there.*

Instinctively, I knew he was talking about one of my past lives, and additional clues from the dream seemed to point to my incarnation as an eighth-century nun, when I received my education in the diocese of Salisbury.

But the next day, out of the blue, I decided to investigate a much earlier life that was tied to Stonehenge. A day later, I noticed my son Geoffrey (then six years old) working on a project with great care and intent. He cut a large rectangle from a piece of paper. Inside the rectangle, he drew a yellow spiral with a tail at the end that formed the letter "e." As I looked on, he grabbed a gray crayon and began coloring the background.

"What's that?" I asked.

"It's an ancient spiral," he said.

For a moment, I was dumbstruck. I'd never mentioned such a thing to him and couldn't think where he'd heard of the concept of the sacred spiral.

"I did it for you," he continued. "You can keep it by the computer when you're working. I'm coloring it gray and made it a rectangle so it looks like a stone. An ancient stone."

"What's the 'e' for?" I questioned.

"I don't know," he replied. "I just wanted it to have one."

I wondered if it stood for "England" or "energy."

Roughly two weeks later, my editor mentioned that a new henge had been discovered near Stonehenge. Stonehenge is near Salisbury, and I couldn't help linking the news to my dream.

Did the robed figure's words "another one" refer to the other henge that was found? Had I lived there long ago? The clue might even point to a life in Old Sarum, because its inhabitants eventually moved to another location, the river valley site that became Salisbury.

Whatever the case, synchronicity was afoot. The clue from my dream, my son's project, and the newly discovered henge worked together to boost my interest and keep me digging.

Postscript: A few days after writing the previous passage, I read an Associated Press article concerning British researchers' latest theory about Stonehenge. They believed a larger stone circle built 500 years before Stonehenge at that same site had served as a communal graveyard. Could that be the "other one" to which the robed figure had referred?

Next, here's an example in which the synchronicity of events became clear years after they occurred and only when my research focused in on a specific lifetime. I had no idea just how connected the incidents were while they were happening.

In 1988, during my semester abroad in London, my roommates—Peggy and Susan—and I traveled to Bavaria over spring break. I'll never forget our drive from Switzerland back to our German hotel. We were on an alpine road in the middle of a blizzard. Whitney Houston belted out her latest hit on the radio, but Susan and Peggy ignored her for more pressing concerns. Our rented Fiat lacked snow tires, and the icy road's microscopic shoulder was invisible in the vortex of winter's fury.

From the back seat, I observed my roommates' stress with detachment. It might've been a chocolate high from the half-eaten, foot-long Milka bar in my lap, but something assured me we'd be all right.

Peggy, a lifelong Christian, gripped the steering wheel and began to pray. Her murmured words seemed automatic, almost unconscious, because her whole being was focused on survival. Suddenly, the snow thinned, and she spotted a dark, wooden cross at the top of a hill. Heavy snowfall resumed a moment later, but despite that shroud, sporadic glimpses of the cross led her up the mountain to the safety of our hotel.

The cross hadn't been there before. It was newly planted in the exact location we needed, and it was the perfect symbol to inspire Peggy's trust. Its appearance might not have been supernatural, but it was definitely the answer to a prayer.

That night, I had a peculiar dream. I was walking down a brightly lit hallway toward a large, gilded cross. Two women—one on either side of me—were my sisters, in the monastic sense of the word. We marveled at the light, which for some reason wasn't supposed to be there. But it felt as sacred as our holy vows and the bond we shared with one another.

As part of that same vacation, my roommates and I traveled to Italy. Rome was cool, but Tuscany inspired me the most. After sightseeing in Florence, I had a strange experience upon waking in our hotel room. For a brief moment, I glimpsed a wooden cross at the foot of my bed and a ghost standing at my right side, gazing down at me. I've never been sure whether it was a dream or a vision, but I now believe it was yet another clue to a past life.

Besides those "dreams" and our death-defying journey through the blizzard, one other memory from the trip stands out. One night, huddled against the icy blasts of yet another snowstorm, my roommates and I met an American guy who was also studying abroad. He excused himself for a moment to use a pay phone, and as he spoke German into the receiver, it hit me: I, too, would study that language, and it would lead me to my future.

The next academic year, I studied German at the University of Aberdeen in Scotland. When I returned to FSU for my senior year, I continued my German studies and competed for a Fulbright Scholarship to study at a graduate school in Germany. I listed Heidelberg University as my intended school, not because of any particular coursework, but because the name "Heidelberg" just sounded right.

Only one student could receive the prize, though, and the Fulbright committee chose me as an alternate. Heidelberg University wasn't in the cards after all. Crestfallen, I considered my future. I was so sure the German language held the seed of my future studies.

Actually, it did, just not in the way I expected. One month before I graduated from FSU, my German professor remarked on my ear for languages and innate talent for phonetics. A fellow student overheard him and mentioned that his father was a professor at the University of Wisconsin-

Madison. According to him, the university had a great linguistics department.

My professor lit up like a child on Christmas morning. "That sounds like a perfect match for you, Judy, if you want it."

All of a sudden, I did want it. It seemed the most natural thing in the world to switch my focus from historic events to the communication that supported them. My fellow German student called his father that night, and a few days later, my application to UW-Madison arrived in the mail.

Soon after, I was accepted into the Linguistics Department's graduate school. Little did I know that a woman I'd known in England and Germany 1,200 years earlier was already studying linguistics there.

It took two decades for the events that occurred during spring break of 1988—including the prompt toward the German language—to reveal their synchronistic nature. By that time, I was heavy into my research of past lives, and experiential clues pointed to one, if not several, lifetimes as a nun.

I didn't have specifics, so I started with the clue of my birthday, April 30. On my twenty-fifth birthday, I learned that Sweden's *Valborgsafton* and Germany's *Walpurgisnacht*—celebrated on that selfsame date—were named for the eighth-century English-born nun St. Walburga. She also inspired May Day traditions in Bavaria. At that point, all I knew about the woman herself was that she was an Anglo-Saxon nun who'd lived in England and Germany. I didn't think I'd been Walburga in a past life, but I knew that I was somehow linked with her. Research beckoned.

Walburga was born in Devon, the capital of which is Exeter.

Hmm ... I lived on Exeter Street for the first eighteen years of my life, I thought, *and I definitely experienced a taste of the supernatural in Devon.*

A wooden cross was erected on her family's land, and she and her father, Richard, her mother, Wuna (Winna), and her brothers, Willibald and Winnebald (Wynnebald)—all of whom became saints—said their daily prayers in front of it.

I know those names, I thought. *I knew those men. In Italy, I saw a wooden cross at the foot of my bed. And it was a wooden cross that led me and my roommates to safety during that German blizzard.*

Supposedly, a great storm arose during Walburga's voyage to Germany. The sea raged around the boat, and several aboard panicked. Not Walburga. She knelt on the deck and prayed, and as the story goes, the ocean instantly calmed. The sailors proclaimed it a miracle when they reached dry land.

I had my own stormy journey into Germany, I thought, *but I wasn't afraid. Was my inexplicable sense of calm due to subconscious knowledge of Walburga's safe crossing?*

One alleged event at Walburga's abbey in Heidenheim involved her fellow nuns fetching her for supper one evening. The hallway leading to her room was filled with a "divine" light that remained until the next morning.

Does that explain the dream I had in Germany of the mysterious light in a monastic setting? I wondered. *Even if the event didn't actually occur, I might've known the story.*

That's when a quotation from a female author of the period leapt from the computer screen: "No one ever again shall say it is all nonsense."

A tingling sensation washed over my scalp.

I know that, I thought. *I wrote it.*

In fact, that sentiment was partly why I penned this book. Time and again, throughout my life, I've felt compelled to discuss spiritual/paranormal events with anyone who's interested. But I always sensed—even from the time I was a little girl—that I was closest to Spirit and could serve God best when I wrote. The woman quoted seemed to be wired the same way. At different times, in different places, we shared a common goal: to serve Spirit by expanding awareness through the written word.

Her narratives demonstrated the common desire of all pilgrims to travel to sacred sites. She also suggested the concept of sacred time (the eternal now) by showing how present places opened windows to the past. That rang a few bells!

The author was an Anglo-Saxon nun named Hygeburg (Hugeberc). She was Walburga's kinswoman, although no one knows exactly how they were related. She, too, traveled from England to Germany (although several years later) and lived at the Bavarian double monastery of Heidenheim am Hahnenkamm, which Willibald and Winnebald—both of whom were monks—had founded in 752.

When I read that, I recalled another trip to Germany while I was still in college. My parents were my tour guides, especially in Würzburg, the city known as the "doorway to Bavaria." In fact, they'd cemented their relationship in Würzburg while dating and returned there for their honeymoon. We stayed in the same hotel they had on both occasions, and twenty years later, so did my older brother, Billy. Travel to Bavaria was definitely a family affair!

I read on. Around 778, Hygeburg wrote a *vita* (life) of both of her kinsmen, Willibald and Winnebald, reporting their travels and the miraculous events associated with them. She claimed authorship of the *vitae* through a cryptogram (a linguistic riddle), so no one knew she wrote them until the secret writing was decoded in 1931. Interesting that she and I not only wrote about supernatural/spiritual events, but were both drawn to linguistics.

Her kinsmen's father, Richard, died in Lucca, a Tuscan city northwest of Florence. One source claimed that Hygeburg died there too, at a much later date. Did their deaths have anything to do with the ghost I perceived at my bedside in Florence? Funny that Hygeburg traveled from England to Germany and Italy, and I did too during spring break of 1988.

I considered the words "Hygeburg" and "Heidenheim" and remembered my impulsive decision to study at Heidelberg University. No wonder the name sounded right! Had I not been drawn toward the German language, I might never have studied linguistics or moved to Wisconsin, where I became friends with a woman who had once been Walburga.

I didn't know it at the time, but all of the "paranormal" events of that one trip during spring break were clues to my life as Hygeburg. The dream, the wooden crosses that appeared in Bavaria and Florence, the intuitive nudge toward the German language: all are examples of synchronicity at work.

Apparitions/visitations and synchronicity are extraordinary experiences that remind us of our spiritual nature and sometimes indicate what our spirits are up to in lives beyond our present reality. When they enter your experience, embrace the moment, pay attention, and see what comes of it.

9

HISTORICAL RESEARCH

Few, if any, of your past-life identities will be famous historical figures. Still, it does happen, in which case you are blessed to have a wealth of recorded history at your fingertips! Fortunately, records aren't reserved just for history's celebrities. Everyday individuals show up on numerous documents, many of which can be accessed through websites like Ancestry.com. And if you have the opportunity to travel to locations that match up with your past lives, do so, by all means. There are a lot of records—along with local legends, which are sometimes telling—unavailable elsewhere.

When most people think of history, events and personages spring to mind. Yet language can be just as important to past-life research. Be it a foreign language, a "dead" language, or simply a peculiarity of speech in your native tongue (e.g., spontaneous use of an old-fashioned or archaic expression that isn't part of your known vocabulary), you can investigate it.

A single word could inspire research. Over a period of six months, when Connor was two, he repeatedly used an unusual word to describe how I wound my hair up and into a barrette at the back of my head. It wasn't a bun, exactly, but more like a donut twist that shot out at the top like the leaves of a palm tree. The term he used, seemingly as a noun and a verb, was *masse*. I use that spelling because his pronunciation of the "a" was closer to the French vowel than to the English "æ" in "mass."

When I sported the hairdo, he touched it with fascination. "Mommy *masse*," he said, his voice and smile oozing a mixture of awe and contentment.

When my hair hung freely down my back, he protested. "No, no. Mommy *masse*, please. Mommy go up, please."

The word "mass" entered the English language around 1400, from the Old French *masse*, "lump" (eleventh century), and the Latin *massa*, "kneaded dough or lump." But it wasn't used as a verb—meaning "to gather into a clump or mass"—in England until about 1563.

Connor used the word as both a noun and a verb. So if he plucked it from a past life in England, it would've been around or after the 1560s. More clues were necessary, of course, but it was a good start.

Intuition could spark your historical research. So could a person's random comments or incongruous behavior. All of these things prompted research into my past life in fifteenth-century Ireland.

Despite the wealth of experience that suggested at least one past life there, the puzzle remained unsolved. That is, until one afternoon shortly after our sons' fifth birthday. They were sitting at the dining room table coloring, when Connor abandoned his artwork and sidled over to the bookshelf.

He ran his fingers along the book spines and paused over one of them. Then he pulled the book from the shelf and held it up to me. It was the same picture book of Ireland that had inspired my first trip overseas.

He flipped through it, then stopped midway through and stared at one of the pages. His rapt attention sparked my curiosity, so I moved to stand beside him. Laying a hand on his shoulder, I looked down at a full-page photo of Donegal Castle. According to the caption, it was built by the O'Donnells and completed around 1474. It was also one of the images that had filled my heart with longing when I was seventeen.

"Mommy," Connor said, "do you remember when you were a princess in that castle?"

Nonplussed, I turned to him. "What?" I asked.

"You lived in that castle when you were a princess," he said, pointing, "a long time ago."

"Why do you say that, honey?" I ventured.

He looked deeply into my eyes. "Because I know."

Three hours later, when Dan came home from work, Connor raced to meet him at the front door. "Daddy, Daddy," he said, grabbing Dan's hand. "Come look at this picture."

He led Dan to the dining room table, where the picture book lay closed. In a flash, Connor had it open to the same page he'd shown me before.

"See that castle?" Connor said. "Mommy was a princess there a long time ago."

Dan turned to look at me. All I could do was shrug.

"Why do you say that?" Dan asked.

"Because she was," Connor answered. "It's the truth."

I knew Ireland had its own aristocracy, but I'd always associated royalty with English or Scottish monarchs. Obviously, my knowledge of Irish history was limited, and it's possible that other English lifetimes had influenced my preconception. Perhaps that's what some preconceptions are: thoughts conceived in—or because of—previous lives.

A memory from college stirred in my mind. I was eating lunch with a new friend, and midway through the meal, she asked, "Is that really how you eat? It's so dainty."

I thought she was kidding. I had a passion for food, and "dainty" was the last word I would've used to describe my relationship with it.

"No, I'm serious," she said. "You eat like a princess."

Now, standing beside my husband and children in a dining room littered with coloring books and broken crayons, I brushed the memory aside.

Ridiculous, I thought. *Even if there were Irish princesses at some point in history, what are the odds I was one of them?*

We dropped the subject. Soon afterward, a migraine crept into the right side of my head. Apparently, the right side of the body is associated with conscious thought and the left side, the subconscious. Who knows? Maybe the passage of past-life information from my subconscious to my conscious mind created a stir.

By the time we started the boys' bedtime ritual, my head was pounding without restraint. Connor sat on his bed, and I knelt on the floor in front of him. Although I hadn't mentioned where I hurt, he reached toward my head and placed his palm on the exact spot that throbbed the most.

Then he slipped out of bed, moved behind me, and ran his fingers through my hair. Finally, he placed his hands on my shoulders. Within thirty seconds, the headache dissolved, and relief flooded through me.

When asked how he'd made the headache go away, Connor replied, "I moved it around and made it better." I guessed he was referring to the blocked energy.

He stood in front of me again, and for the second time, he placed his hands on my shoulders. His gaze locked with mine, and his expression turned almost fatherly. I had the bizarre feeling he was proud of me.

My intuition told me that moment was connected with what he'd said about the princess in the castle. A little research—about the O'Donnells and Donegal Castle—was in order. That's when I happened upon the name Nuala O'Connor Faly.

"Nuala" is short for Fionnula/Finnghuala/Finola. A memory from high school flashed before me of the first time I saw actress Finola Hughes's name across the TV screen. She was a good actress and a great dancer, but—though I'd never understood why—it was her name that entranced me.

Now I looked up the meaning of Finola: "bright/fair-shouldered." A chill ran through me as I remembered Connor's fingers running through my blond hair and how he'd deliberately placed his hands on my shoulders...twice.

At that point, I had to read everything I could find on Nuala O'Connor Faly, for I sensed a deep connection between us. I was flabbergasted to learn she could've been considered a princess for several reasons. Her father was Calvagh O'Connor Faly (known as Baron of Offaly), a chieftain descended from Cathaoir Mor, King of Ireland in the second century. Her mother, Margaret, was the daughter of Tiege O'Carroll, King of Ely. Her first husband, Niall Garv O'Donnell, was a chieftain known as the King of Tir Conaill. Her second husband was Hugh Boy O'Neill, Chief or Prince of Clannaboy.

She gave her first husband four sons, the second of whom was Hugh Roe O'Donnell. A couple of secondary sources confused that son with her two husbands and so listed her as Hugh Roe's wife, but I instinctively knew the information was false. Subsequent research in historical annals proved she was indeed Hugh Roe's mother.

All at once, I remembered a mystery from my childhood. From the moment my little brother, Bobby, was born, he seemed as much my son as my sibling. I adored him and drove my mother crazy because I rarely used his "real" name; instead, I called him what she could only assume was a combination of the words "babe" (the archaic form of baby) and "you." In a startling moment of clarity, I now realized what I'd really been saying: "Babe Hugh."

Then I thought back to my fascination with the name Finola Hughes. Finola and Hugh!

Nuala's son, Hugh Roe, married another Nuala: Nuala O'Brien of Munster.

The principal residence for the O'Briens (kings and later earls of Thomond) was Bunratty Castle. Post-Cromwell, the

O'Briens also built a beautiful residence at Dromoland Castle. Had Lady Nuala visited her daughter-in-law's family in that area?

Was that why I booked the tower room of Dromoland Castle for my honeymoon? Did it explain my emotional experience in Bunratty's dungeon? Also, the first time I spoke Irish in my sleep was roughly two hours after my parents and I arrived in Ireland ... in a bed and breakfast in the village of Bunratty, not five minutes from the castle itself.

As soon as I read the name of Nuala's first husband, Niall Garv O'Donnell, I was certain of two things: (1) Nuala's family had forced her to marry him because it was an advantageous alliance, but after a time, a deep and abiding friendship blossomed between them; and (2) Dan had been Niall Garv. Then it hit me ... when the two of us peered down into the pit of Bunratty's dungeon, some kind of alchemical reaction freed the painful memories from our shared past.

So ... why the intensity of emotion? In 1435, Niall Garv O'Donnell was captured by the English and imprisoned in London. Four years later, he was moved to the Isle of Man, where he died in captivity in 1439. Upon reading this, three puzzle pieces clicked into place: (1) Dan's dislike for enclosed spaces, particularly when crowded by two or more people; (2) his spontaneous vision—during meditation one night—of a flag with the Cross of St. George flying atop an English ship that he intuitively connected to Ireland; and (3) the reason why the thought of Dan popped into my head in Colonial Williamsburg as I stared at an aged British flag.

As if the capture, imprisonment, and death of a husband weren't reason enough for tears, in 1456, Nuala's eldest son,

Donall O'Donnell (then King of Tir Conaill) was murdered at the same time her second son, Hugh Roe, was taken prisoner.

In 1447, Nuala became a Franciscan nun at Killeagh Abbey in Tullamore. Suddenly, my impressions inside the fifteenth-century ruin of the Franciscan abbey at Muckross made sense. During that same trip to Ireland, while traveling south from Kylemore Abbey to Galway on a tour bus, I had felt an inexplicable desire to travel north.

Donegal Castle, which Connor pinpointed in the picture book, is definitely north of Galway. So are the ruins of the Franciscan abbey of Ross-Errily near Tuam. Apparently, Nuala traveled there in 1474 while the Franciscan order was holding a general chapter. Attended by a brilliant escort, including many "gallow-glasses" (armed retainers or mercenaries), she interrupted their deliberations. She requested—then insisted—that they establish their order in the principality of Tir Conaill. Then, with a band of Franciscans, she journeyed to Donegal, where the Franciscan friary was founded around the same time as the new castle.

Nuala must've stayed with her son, Hugh Roe, and his wife in Donegal for at least a short spell, if only to recover from the Ross-Errily adventure. That would explain why Connor envisioned the "princess" in the new castle. Either that or he received an impression of the O'Donnells' earlier home in the Lough Eske area outside Donegal Town.

Perhaps Nuala's connection with the Franciscans explains why every psychic I've consulted since the boys' births has mentioned St. Francis hanging around me. He is said to promote the discovery of one's life purpose, spiritual devotion, and communication with animals, all of which apply to my experience. One famous event from his life involved his interaction with a wolf, an animal that has been a frequent visitor in my dreams since childhood. St. Francis was also known to communicate with birds, and I've received quite a few messages from those (particularly ravens and hawks) as well.

A year before I knew Nuala existed, the distinguished psychic team I've mentioned before told me that I had a happy life as a nun outside of Dublin in the fifteenth century. Killeagh Abbey in Tullamore—where Nuala took the veil—is about an hour from Dublin. They also said that Connor and Geoffrey had inspired me and Dan with the names we gave them. Why? Were their names meant to be breadcrumbs leading us to the discovery of past lives? Perhaps my son (Connor) in this lifetime was my father (Calvagh O'Connor Faly) in a previous one.

The *Annals of the Four Masters* figured largely in my research, and they were compiled at Donegal's monastery, the same monastery Nuala strove to establish. It's amazing to think that I was directly responsible for a monastery that allowed my present self to research my past self! It's as if my soul planned it that way...

If any of your spirit guides played a role in one of your past lives, you can check historic records for information about them. You'll gain insight into your own past life and how it affects your current one.

The first time I saw my spirit guide Black Hawk in meditation, we were inside a cabin in the woods. Water trickled nearby, and I had a vision of two trees with roots entwined. As I stared into Black Hawk's piercing, black eyes, I felt a powerful maternal love for him. I knew that he was either my son or someone I regarded as a son. I felt proud of him and saw that pride reflected back at me. He was pleased with my spiritual progress, even though I doubted whether I'd made any.

Years later, when I looked into that lifetime and discovered that Black Hawk did in fact exist, I discovered quite a lot through research. Black Hawk spoke Meskwaki-Sauk, an Algonquian language. He was close to both of his parents, and at his father's death, he inherited "the great medicine bag" of his forefathers. His eyes were described as exceptionally black and piercing, just as they had appeared in my meditation!

He was a member of the Thunder Clan and the great-grandson of Nanamakee ("Thunderer"), who was a principal chief among the Sauk. He even named one of his sons "Whirling Thunder." Could that be another reason—apart from my life as Thorgunna and the connection to Thor—why I reveled in thunderstorms?

According to oral history, the Sauk originated on the Atlantic Coast near the Saint Lawrence Seaway in Canada. Then they migrated, first to Michigan, then west to Wisconsin, and on to the Upper Mississippi River Valley. Black Hawk was born in the Indian village of Saukenuk on the Rock and Mississippi Rivers in what became Illinois. At the time, Saukenuk was the economic and religious center of the Sauk world, with an estimated population of 11,000. It was arranged in lots, blocks, and streets around a village square, and families lived in long log houses. I'd always loved longhouses, whether First Nations or Native American.

Supposedly, a protective spirit lived in a cave on the island that served as the people's garden. Eyewitnesses said it had white wings like a huge swan. When I read that, I couldn't help but think of the "giant owls" my children observed in our home. Geoffrey had even seen them watching me—and heard the word "hawk"—while I researched Black Hawk's life.

The Sauk men hunted. The women worked in the maize fields.

I recalled the first time I stepped foot in a corn field at age thirty-three. Dan and I had traveled to Pennsylvania to celebrate our first wedding anniversary. I skipped through the rows, running my hands along the stalks in a moment of pure joy. With perhaps more force than was seemly, I hugged Dan and thanked him for giving me the best anniversary present in the world.

I felt utterly alive and at home inside the "maize maze," but my reaction didn't compute. Now, it finally made sense.

Like many Native American tribes, the Sauk stressed the importance of place. They believed Saukenuk was located at the intersection of four cosmic layers above and below the earth, which translated into fertility and abundance for its people.

Until I married Dan, a similar idea ruled my decisions; the place where I lived—actually, the way it felt—was crucial to my well-being. Jobs came and went, and there were always new friends to meet. But the land itself was all-important. Maybe that's why I was so ripe for my first healing in Wales.

Black Hawk's refusal to vacate tribal territory resulted in the Black Hawk War of 1832, during which he led a band of men, women, and children into Wisconsin. Wisconsin was also where he'd first visited me in spirit.

He ended his days in Iowa, living quietly with his wife in a cabin along the Des Moines River. Nearby was Black Hawk's Spring, and get this: it flowed beneath the interlaced roots of two trees, an ash and an elm—two trees with roots intertwined!

As you can see, historical research will give you a world of information and help you connect your experiences in this life with those from other lives. Above all, listen to your inner monologue (or dialogue!) while doing your research. Sometimes it's your soul talking; other times it's your angels and spirit guides directing your discoveries. Either way, the thoughts that pop into your head will provide clues and confirmation that literally bring history to life.

10

INPUT FROM ANGELS AND OTHER GUIDING SPIRITS

Remember, time is an illusion, and the soul is omniscient. Recalling past lives is really just connecting with your soul, which is in and around all of your incarnations at once. Angels and other guiding spirits also operate beyond time-bound awareness, so they're a good source of information about past lives. They know details of your previous identities, present life, and potential futures.

Your spirit guides studied your other incarnations once they agreed to guide your current one. They consulted your many "charts" (pre-birth plans for any given lifetime) and the akashic records, which include "histories" of how those lives played out. In addition, some guides might've played key roles—even friends or family members—in your past lives.

On the angel front, your guardian angel is a boundless source of information. It was created from your soul's essence and is the same for every one of your lifetimes. In other words, your guardian angel is present with each "you" in every moment. Archangel Azrael, aka the Angel of Death, can also help with past-life exploration.

You'll receive input from angels and other guiding spirits in one of two ways. Either they'll initiate contact, in which case stuff just happens, or you'll make the effort.

Spirit-Initiated Guidance

As previously mentioned, angels and other spirits can guide your discoveries and fill you in on past-life details through your inner monologue during historical research. But there are countless other ways they'll steer you in the right direction, mostly via the psychic "clairs" we discussed in chapter 2. They might target your dreams; after all, that's when your defenses—preconceived notions and conditioned responses— are most likely to be down. You might even be able to research and confirm the information you receive.

A word to the wise: if your angels and guides suggest that you go somewhere or do something specific, there's a good reason for it. In August 1993, my flight from Sweden back to the States had a three-hour layover in Iceland's Keflavík International Airport, just outside of Reykjavík. I remained in the airport for the duration, but I couldn't shake the curious murmur of destiny—and a spirit guide's whisper—that tickled my ears.

*This place is important. Not Keflavík or Reykjavík, but far-
ther out. One day, you must return.*

I promised myself I would, although nearly seven years
passed before I honored that promise. The journey had to
wait for the right time and the right companion: my husband,
Dan. Shortly after I moved in with him, I dreamed of a spirit
guide I'd never seen before. She was an Indian woman dressed
in an orange sari, and in the dream, I trailed her along numerous passageways through an airport. Finally, she stopped in
front of a giant window, and I followed her gaze.

Out on the tarmac, an airplane waited at the end of the
gate. Any minute, it would taxi to the runway and take off. I
couldn't identify its destination, but I knew it was someplace
cold. I also gathered the Indian woman wanted me to travel
there.

Is this just a dream? I wondered.

As if she'd heard my thoughts, the woman turned to face
me. She didn't blink, not once. Her round, dark eyes fixed
upon mine until all doubt was erased. Our meeting was as
real as they come, and I had the definite sense she knew me
better than I knew myself.

Two words came to me, both of which I assumed were
names: *Ananda* and *Samara*. When I woke, I hit the Internet
for answers. *Samara* is of Hebrew and Arabic origin and has
three meanings: "guardian," "protected by God," and "night
talk." *Ananda* is a Sanskrit name that means "ultimate bliss."

At the time, I couldn't pinpoint the cold land my guide had
indicated, but about a month later—with no knowledge of my
dream—Dan suggested we travel to Iceland. His willingness
to make the trip in the dead of winter confirmed what I'd

come to believe as truth: I had met my match. Here was a fellow fan of wind and snow. Here, too, was the bearded man I'd known and loved in a distant but distinct dreamtime. The hammer of the gods, forged in fire and ice, had pounded on memory and mood until it was heard. It had facilitated our reunion; now it summoned us home.

While in Iceland, we spent three days in Akureyri, the "capital of the north." The snow was deep and the wind was fierce, which translated to lonely stretches of road where our rental car was the only vehicle around. Still, we carried on. One afternoon as we drove along, the clouds parted, allowing a shaft of light to illuminate a giant shape in the distance.

It might've been a volcanic hill, but it had the aura and majesty of a mountain. Its relatively flat top was rounded at the edges, which softened its otherwise looming presence high above the snow-covered plateau. We nicknamed it "Valhalla," because it attracted the only ray of light for miles around and because its brilliance was almost blinding to eyes now accustomed to leaden skies.

Those skies remained our constant companion as we explored numerous craters and towering lava formations around Lake Mývatn, but whenever "Valhalla" came into view, it shone like a beacon. We had to laugh. It seemed preposterous that the sun should ignore every feature of the landscape but one.

In Norse mythology, Valhalla was the great hall where the souls of heroes slain in battle spent eternity. In common English usage, it was a perfect destiny or paradise, not unlike the popular use of the Sanskrit word *nirvana*.

In my dream about the airport, the Indian spirit guide had whispered another Sanskrit word: *ananda*, or "ultimate bliss." That same dream had pointed me toward travel in a wintry place and had given me the word *samara*, one meaning of which was "night talk."

That night, in our Akureyri hotel room, a strange sound woke me. I rolled over in bed to stare at its source.

Dan was talking in his sleep, but not in English. It was a Scandinavian tongue, similar to Icelandic, and I almost understood it. I felt right on the verge, like when a word or thought is on the tip of your tongue. Given a slight, indefinable shift, I would've comprehended it.

All at once, I knew. He was speaking Old Norse.

I didn't wake him, and after a couple of minutes, he stopped. But his easy pronunciation and fluency stayed with me.

Dan always said he was terrible with languages. Well, not with this one. The authority of his speech echoed in my mind, replacing my sense of wonder with the power of certainty. What some would judge impossible seemed not only possible, but appropriate. Factor in my dreams and past experiences, as well as Dan's lifelong desire to see Iceland, and the event borders on predictable, just another piece of the puzzle we were meant to find. I believe my spirit guide knew that once Dan and I traveled to Iceland together, he would speak Old Norse in his sleep, and it would be yet another past-life connection that involved us both.

As you can see, angels and other spirits nudge us toward experiences that enlighten us. They encourage self-knowledge, which includes information about your whole self, i.e., your soul and its many components (lives).

Long before I researched Black Hawk's life, I dreamed I was standing at my kitchen counter, sorting clusters of herbs.

The cabinet at face level opened to reveal a raccoon. It jumped onto the counter, looked me in the eye, and scratched my hand. Abruptly, I awoke, certain the dream was important.

With a little research, I learned that the word "raccoon" was thought to derive from the Algonquian Indian word *arckunem*, which meant "hand-scratcher," and raccoons sometimes symbolized disguise. I now believe Black Hawk sent the raccoon to me as a messenger that saw through my present "disguise" (my identity in this life) and reminded me of a past life in which I spoke the Algonquian language of Meskwaki-Sauk and used herbal medicine to help others.

Often, what angels and guides reveal to you alters your perspective and holds you to the spiritual path you chose for yourself before you reincarnated. There was a period of about a week when I considered giving up on this book. At the end of that week, I piddled around on the computer and decided to enter a few online sweepstakes. The process required typing preselected code words to complete the entries, and as I entered one after another, I began to feel a connection: "birthday girl" (my birthday was the following day), "in limbo," "writing desk," "story," "have purpose," "keep going," "been there," "England," "France." Several times, the term "pin money" popped up. I knew it was an old expression, but the fact that it kept appearing made me wonder if it was a message from my angels and guides.

I looked into the history of the term, and one source said it originated in Tudor England. Apparently, while Katherine Howard was queen, she introduced pins into England from France. At first, the pins were expensive luxury items, so husbands set aside a specific sum for their wives to buy them.

In one fell swoop, I learned more about a past life and was encouraged to keep writing this book. But angels and once-human spirit guides weren't the only helpers in town. Since childhood, my writing has been guided by another type of spirit: the animal totem Spider.

Numerous times as a child, I woke in the morning with spider bites on my head. I had long, fine hair, so it was all too easy for eight-legged explorers to become entangled. Perhaps they had to bite their way free. Yet I've come to realize that spiders—whether they appear in dreams or the "real" world—have always been a message from Spirit urging me to write.

This brings up an important point: one of the best tools for uncovering past lives is the written word—not just what you read in your research, but what you write. I've been blessed with a good memory, but for most of my life, I've also kept records of my experience through journals, detailed letters, and creative projects. Maybe you've done the same, but even if you haven't, you can start now.

Write down everything you remember from childhood to the present that could relate to past lives. And from now on, when you have an experience that seems supernatural, write (or type) it down! If you hate writing with a passion that burns brighter than a supernova, then record memos on your computer, use a digital recorder, or dust off that forgotten tape recorder.

Record the details, even if they seem trivial. It may be years before you understand their significance, but if you note them now, you'll have a ready-made reference when the time is right.

Making the Effort

One of the easiest ways to communicate with angels and spirit guides is through "automatic dictation." You seek information from your spirit(s) of choice and consciously write down the answers you receive. You can do this alone or with a friend or spouse, in which case one of you asks the questions aloud and writes down—or types—the other's responses.

You can call on a specific spirit, e.g., your guardian angel, Archangel Azrael, or a spirit guide you know by name. Or you can just call on your "angels, guardians, and guides" in general and learn from them.

Channel/psychic medium Kim O'Neill refers to this technique as "channeling." She believes that angels and guides are responsible for as much as 80 to 85 percent of the information flowing through our brains, and in her audio CD *Communicating With Your Angels*, she gives easy directions for accessing it. This method can provide answers and advice about most any subject, as well as information about other incarnations. I'll add only two steps to O'Neill's method, and they will appear in italics.

(1) Set aside a 30–45-minute block of time at least once a week for channeling.

(2) Prepare a list of questions you'd like answered.

(3) At the appointed time, go to a quiet place, even if it's just inside your parked car.

(4) Close your eyes. Take a deep breath, then let it out completely.

(5) *Imagine white light pouring down on you from above so that it fills you and encases you in a bubble of divine love and protection. Then ask your angels, guardians, and*

guides—either in general or using specific names—to join you and help you receive the most accurate information possible.

(6) Say aloud, "Brain, shut off."

(7) Speak your first question out loud and listen for an answer. It will appear, usually within five to ten seconds, as thoughts in your mind or an actual voice. Record any response you "hear." Continue with your other questions, posing them in your mind or out loud. Toward the end of the session, give the angels an open floor, i.e., a chance to tell you whatever they want you to know.

(8) *Thank the angels or whomever you contacted for the information you received.*

And that's it. At first, you might feel like you're talking to yourself or that some of the responses are merely wishful thinking. If you're unsure whether the answers are coming from you or the angels, ask them about it. You can also experiment with channeling at different times during the day to determine when you "hear" the best. At first, you might pick up only short replies, like "yes," "no," "1892," or "blond." But soon, the answers will flesh out with details that will surprise you and your channeling partner, if you have one.

Be patient with yourself and the process. With time and practice, you'll gain confidence in your abilities. You might even use words or phrases that aren't part of your known vocabulary. As you confirm information—names, dates, and details about historical events or "foreign" cultures—through subsequent research, your trust will blossom. And, of course, the more positive your thoughts and mindset are, the easier it will be to hear the voice(s) of your angels, guardians, and guides.

11

INPUT FROM PROFESSIONALS

Sooner or later, you're bound to consider the help of a
past-life regressionist or a reputable psychic. You don't
need them to recall past lives, but they can certainly facili-
tate and/or validate your investigation.

PAST-LIFE REGRESSION

Past-life regression is one way to revisit other lifetimes. If it
interests you, there are a plethora of certified hypnotists and
clinical hypnotherapists who can help. During a regression,
the psychic senses that serve you most—clairvoyance,
clairaudience, clairsentience, etc.—will influence your experience and help you hone in on sights, sounds, physical sensations, etc., as you remember past-life events. I say "remember,"

but in reality, your consciousness simply shifts gears to let you access what your soul is experiencing elsewhere.

During grad school, I decided to confront my snake phobia and sought the help of a hypnotherapist. She "put me under," and I immediately found myself in a past life as a young woman in Ireland. The impromptu regression could've been an attempt to escape my fears, since the last ice age had rendered Ireland a snake-free zone. Perhaps the lifetime impacted my phobia in some way.

Regardless, I was instantly aware of my past-life self's plight. My family wanted me to marry an older, wealthy man, and the mere idea of such a union disgusted me. I felt trapped by expectations and thought I could avoid the marriage by becoming a nun, which would give me some semblance of independence. Yet I feared that my parents' control and my intended's influence would win the day.

We lived in a cottage, but I had left it to walk alone in the woods and collect my thoughts. The autumn air was crisp, and with each step, my feet crunched the dry leaves that carpeted the ground. When I reached the lakeshore, I stopped and stared at the tiny rock island across the water. I knew it was only a matter of time before someone came looking for me, so I had to return and face my future head-on. I spun on my heel but halted mid-turn. With the lake to my right, the woods to my left, and an overgrown outcrop behind me, I took a deep breath and soaked up one final moment of freedom.

Once the hypnotherapist brought me out of hypnosis, she remarked, "You really seemed to feel your way through the regression." Apparently, I described not only what I saw, but how things felt: the cold wind, the rough tree bark, the scrunch of leaves underfoot, etc. My inclination toward clairsentience was obvious and played a big role in the experience.

A few years later, when I wrote my novel about past lives, I traveled to Ireland for research. While exploring a forest in Killarney, I paused to rest beside a lake. Suddenly, every inch of my skin prickled with recognition. I was standing in the same landscape I'd seen in my regression. In addition, it was the setting for a scene I'd plotted for my novel.

In the book, the protagonist turns from the lake and enters a wood. After a time, she discovers the ruins of the house that was her home 400 years earlier.

My head buzzing, I turned from the water and started into the forest. Before long, I stopped short. My jaw dropped at the sight in front of me.

There, surrounded by trees and invaded by nature, stood the ruins of a house. I skirted the structure in disbelief, questioning all that had passed before. Had I received a premonition of this moment? How could I be living the same event I'd planned for my heroine? Granted, these ruins were newer and smaller than the ones I'd envisioned for the story, but the similarity of circumstance and exact match of place were uncanny. All doubt about my past-life regression dissolved.

PROFESSIONAL PSYCHICS

Prompts

Professional psychics can prompt you toward past-life investigation. They might give you bits of information that you'll be able to flesh out later. The kindling is already there in your subconscious; the psychic provides the spark that, if tended, becomes a flame.

In August of 1993, I moved to Salem, Massachusetts. Early into my job at a New Age store there, I spotted a book on Norse, German, and Anglo-Saxon mysteries. Intrigued, I snatched it from the shelf.

A charge shot through me when I located the section on runes. My heart raced as I examined the symbols of the Elder Futhark (runic alphabet) and the Younger Futhark.

Suddenly, I sensed someone was watching me. I glanced up and the feeling was confirmed. One of the psychics was gazing at me with a dreamy look on her face. I strolled over to her, and she seemed to jerk back to full awareness.

"I just saw the image of you in another life, superimposed over your body," she said. "Your hair was longer and blonder, and you were wearing a long gown with a train at the back and brooches in the front. It was beautiful to see."

Periodically throughout the day, I caught her staring at me with the same faraway expression. "I keep seeing you that way, with the flowing hair and gown," she explained.

By the end of the day, I was more than a little curious about her visions, and I wondered if my study of the runes had triggered them. Intuition told me she'd seen a Scandinavian woman from the Viking era. Subsequent research and experience revealed that she'd seen the part of my soul that was Ota.

Validation

One of the most rewarding aspects about talking to a gifted and reputable psychic is validating your own experience. When they confirm something you suspect is true, you'll know you're not crazy and learn to trust your own psychic senses.

As you may already know, psychics work in different ways. Some use specific tools, such as crystals, runes, or the Tarot to tune in to Spirit. All use intuition and the "clair(s)" they've developed most.

Once during a phone reading, a psychic medium relayed past-life information my paternal grandfather gave her. As his energy surrounded her, she began to cough.

"Excuse me," she said. "Someone is coming forward, and I'm getting smoke. Do you have a grandfather in spirit who smoked a pipe?"

"Yes," I replied.

She described his personality to a T and added, "There's something about a past life on the Isle of Man."

I'd always wanted to go there. I even mentioned it to Cecil Williamson, the man who founded a witchcraft museum on the island, when I met him in Devon. "I wouldn't be surprised if I lived there once," I said.

"You did, absolutely," the psychic asserted. "Your grandfather just gave me that information."

It made sense. I could've lived there for a time as Ota with my husband, Thorgestr. His fleet, which invaded Ireland, was thought to have originated from the Isle of Man.

A few years later, I received even more past-life information from the renowned psychic team I've mentioned before. They used automatic writing to channel Spirit, and within the first few minutes of my phone reading, I asked them what they could tell me about my other lives. Their assertions resonated with me and confirmed things I already suspected.

You've read about many of their validations, but here are a few more. Apparently, I did white magic in the Celtic tradition in England, Ireland, Scotland, and Wales. Besides the life as an Irish nun, I had another in Ireland during which I lived on a farm. I was a female writer in the nineteenth century, "a real bluestocking." I lived in India in the third and the eighteenth centuries as a member of the Brahman caste and a teacher of Hinduism. During one of those lives, Connor was my father; in another, he was an Indian monk. I was an astrologer at Stonehenge and in ancient Egypt. During that Egyptian life-time, Dan was an architect and Connor was an Egyptian priest. Geoffrey was Connor's twin in that life and at least one other. Geoffrey was also a Roman soldier during a life when I was his wife. In seventeenth-century Greece, Connor was a male who was extremely close to his grandmother.

One revelation I didn't expect, but the two women were firm about it. According to them, our whole family had been Pleiadian lightworkers eons ago. I wasn't sure what to think, but the psychics had one heck of a track record for accuracy. Then I remembered a particular conversation with the boys.

Geoffrey had said, "We don't live in England anymore."

Connor added, "We're not in outer space either. We're back on Earth."

Had Connor referred to the neighborhood around the star cluster known as the Pleiades? Or had he simply meant another dimension?

A month later, I had another phone reading, this time with a local psychic. Midway through, she told me she'd been doodling stars since the reading began.

"I've never had this before," she said. "There are a lot of angels around you, but stars keep flashing in front of me too. They're so bright that I'm covering one of my eyes. A name just came to me, and I don't know if it's one or two words. It sounds like Al-Debaran, and it might be the name of a star. Look it up when we're done because it's shining all around you and somehow connected to you and your paranormal experiences."

Afterward, I researched Aldebaran and learned that it's the brightest star in the constellation of Taurus. It makes the bull's eye, and its name means "the follower" in Arabic because it seems to follow the Pleiades across the sky. Dan and I are both Taureans, and the connection to the Pleiades seemed more corroboration than coincidence. Not only can psychics validate your findings, but they often validate each other.

Everything I've shared in this section is the type of information you might receive from a professional psychic. The details can serve as stepping stones to further exploration or as welcome validation of lives you've already uncovered.

12

EXERCISES

This chapter contains several exercises that will help you connect with past lives. It includes three forms of divination and two models for self-hypnosis/meditation. After reading through all of them, choose the ones that feel right to you.

DIVINATION

There are many forms of divination, but three are particularly suited for gleaning past-life information: scrying, pendulum dowsing, and oracle cards. You can employ all three if you feel comfortable doing so, but it's a good idea to ground and cleanse your energy field before beginning any of them. This will help you connect with Earth energy to calm your mind and emotions and clear out any negative energy that could interfere with spiritual/psychic work. Here's a simple exercise you can use to accomplish that.

Grounding and cleansing: Stand with your feet apart. Close your eyes and relax. Take a slow, deep breath and, at the same time, imagine the powerful healing energy of the earth flowing into you through your feet and traveling all the way to the top of your head. It should feel like your inhalation is drawing the earth's energy into you. You can visualize the energy moving upward, hear its deep hum, and/or feel it spreading through your body. Then exhale slowly. Repeat. Inhale again, but this time, as you slowly exhale, imagine a bright white light from above pouring into the top of your head and flowing down through your entire body, washing away all negativity. Repeat.

Once you've grounded and cleansed your energy, you can experiment with the following forms of divination.

Scrying

Scrying is an ancient form of divination that harnesses the psychic sense known as clairvoyance. The seeker gazes into an object—a mirror, a crystal, water, oil, ink, the flame of a candle, etc.—to connect with the spirit world. Since your spirit is part and parcel of that world, scrying can help you glimpse some of the lives your soul embraces.

Late one night, two decades ago, I scried for the first time. Alone in my darkened bedroom, I lit a single candle and placed it atop the table below my mirror. Then I threw a pillow onto the floor and knelt down.

I stared unblinking at my face for several minutes. Before long, a peculiar shift occurred, like the melting of a matrix. It was a dance of light and shadow, of curves and hollows, of features similar to and different from my own. There were blonds and brunettes, women and men. No sooner did I glimpse one than the image shimmered and became another.

How long it continued, I don't know, but it ended with the visage of an older woman with dark, matted hair and dark, round eyes. Her features became so focused and strong, they eclipsed my face completely. She had symmetrical smudges on her cheeks and one across her forehead; whether they were dirt or paint was unclear. The terms "soothsayer" and "keeper of the knowledge" filled my mind, and my intuition whispered that she was from Stone Age Britain.

All at once, I knew she could see me, just as I was seeing her. Was I part of the future she foretold? Was I her future? The power emanating from her was formidable, and as the glimmer in her eyes transformed from curiosity to recognition, I panicked.

I leapt to my feet. Hand on heart, I flicked the closest light switch. Once the comforting glow flooded the room, I turned to face my reflection.

The only woman in the mirror was me.

Many years later, after the aforementioned psychic duo told me I'd been an astrologer at Stonehenge, another psychic concurred and said I'd also been a "reader of the bones." I knew in *my* bones that I'd encountered that ancient part of myself on the first night I scried.

While scrying, the two most important things are to empty your mind of its constant chatter and to be open to whatever might appear. Keep in mind the words of Eckhart Tolle from his book *A New Earth:* "To be still is to be conscious without thought … When you are still, you are who you are beyond your temporal existence: consciousness—unconditioned, formless, eternal." Once you're in touch with that part of yourself, anything is possible.

I suggest using either a regular mirror or a black mirror. If you use the former, you'll stare at your own reflection. If you choose the latter, you could still watch your reflection, but you might have better results if you avoid it by looking at the mirror from an angle. If you perceive the color black as negative, stick with the normal mirror. However, black is a color of power, protection, potential, and the primordial void, so it can act as a gateway to your inner self and your "outer" selves (i.e., past-life identities).

Black mirrors are easy to make. Find or buy an empty picture frame. Any size will do. Remove the glass pane and any cardboard backing. To ensure there are no fingerprints or smudges on the glass, clean both sides of it with glass cleaner. Spread newspaper—or other paper you don't intend to keep—on a flat surface in a well-ventilated area and lay the glass pane (back side up) atop it. Take a can of black spray paint and spray a thin, even coat of paint over the glass. Let it dry for about thirty minutes, then add a second coat of black paint. Once it dries—and if you don't need a third coat of paint—put the glass pane (clear side out) back into the frame. Secure the glass with the cardboard backing, placing it against the painted side of the glass, and double-check that the mirror's surface is clean. Voilà! You've got a black mirror.

You'll want peace and quiet for scrying, so choose a time and place that will give you at least twenty minutes of calm. Then turn off all electric lights. Light two small candles and place one on either side of the mirror. Alternatively, you can have a single lit candle or firelight behind you. If moonlight streams into the room, you might not even need the candles.

Perform the grounding and cleansing exercise described at the beginning of this chapter. Next, set your intention, either through prayer or by stating aloud what you hope to learn. Then call on your angels, guardians, and guides for protection and to help you recall your impressions when you record them afterward. If you're nervous for any reason, call on Archangel Michael to oversee your scrying session. Depending on the mirror's location and your comfort level, you can stand, sit, or kneel. When ready, gaze into the mirror and quiet your thoughts.

The visions may appear in the mirror, in your mind's eye, or in both. Don't be disappointed if nothing happens on your first try, and remain calm and focused when images start to appear. If you freak out, you'll jar yourself from your altered, receptive state. As with most disciplines, fear and impatience will work against you, so relax and muster as much patience as possible. With practice and persistence, you'll open yourself to receive, and the visions will come when the time is right for you. Trust yourself, the process, and the angels, guardians, and guides you've asked to protect you.

Pendulum Dowsing

Dowsing with a pendulum is another way to intuit past-life information. The pendulum could be a crystal, a ring, a metal or wooden pendant, a glass bead, or even a button attached to a small chain, string, or thread that's anywhere from six to twelve inches long. You hold the end of the chain between your thumb and forefinger and allow the pendulum to hang freely. Next, you determine which of the pendant's movements indicate a "yes" and which a "no."

The easiest way to do this is to say, "Show me 'yes.'" Then wait for the pendulum's response. It might move back and forth, sideways, or rotate in a clockwise or counterclockwise direction. Then say, "Show me 'no.'" Observe the corresponding movement. Reaffirm both "yes" and "no" by repeating the above. Finally, test these once more by saying aloud a true statement, such as "My name is Judy," followed by a false statement, such as "My name is Gargamel."

Next, lay a world map—or any map you'd like to use—flat on a table. You can also create a time chart by writing dates on a piece of paper, e.g., 200 BCE/100 BCE/1 CE/100 CE/200 CE and continuing on in both directions: BCE and CE or, if you prefer, BC and AD. Leave at least an inch of empty space between the dates to increase the clarity of your pendulum's answers.

You're ready to roll. Perform the grounding and cleansing exercise given at the beginning of this chapter. Then ask your angels and/or guides to aid your exploration and follow up with the announcement, "I am now connecting with my higher self." Now, select one of the following methods to get started:

(1) For this method, you'll need a straight edge (e.g., a ruler) and a pencil. Position the straight edge so that it lies flat and vertical on the far left side of the map. Hold the hanging

pendulum with one hand and place your free hand on the straight edge. Say aloud, "Give me the location of a past life that's affecting me now. Indicate 'yes' when the straight edge hits the target." Move the vertical straight edge along the map from left to right. Stop when the pendulum indicates "yes" and mark the edge by drawing a straight line with the pencil. Then turn the straight edge so that it's horizontal and move it from the top of the map toward the bottom. Stop when the pendulum again indicates "yes" and mark the edge by drawing another straight line. The point where the two lines intersect is the past-life location.

(2) Hold the pendulum above the center of the map and tell it to point out a continent where you lived a life that's affecting you now. Focus and repeat your direction as many times as necessary. If the pendulum's swing isn't clear or strong, hold it over each continent and ask, "Did I live a past life here that's affecting me now?" Then narrow down the location by country and city.

Once you have your location, double-check it by asking the pendulum if you truly lived there. Be specific; for example, "Did I really live in Stockholm, Sweden?" If the answer is yes, turn your attention to the time chart. Ask aloud when you lived in that location. To determine the date, you can wait for a yes response while doing one of two things: (1) holding the pendulum over each century in turn, or (2) using your free hand to point to each century. Once you've got a century (e.g., 1400 CE), you can narrow down the year with further questions. "Was I born in 1410? In 1420?" etc.

You can learn details of that life by asking more yes or no questions:

"Was I a female in that life?"

"Was I married?"

"Did I have children?"

"Did I believe in God?"

"Was I Christian?"

"Was I rich?"

"Was I literate?"

"Did I earn my living in a trade?"

"Do I know someone from that life in my current life?"

Make your questions as specific as possible, and try to remain neutral. Record your findings. Once you've learned all you want from one life, you can move on to another.

Oracle Cards

If you gravitate toward card decks, you might be interested in oracle cards specifically geared toward past-life exploration. There are several on the market, including *The Phoenix Cards,* the *Symbolon* deck, *Reincarnation Cards: Awakening Far Memory,* and *It's Your Karma Past Life Reincarnation Oracle Card Deck.* All can be used to discover and interpret past-life influences.

I've personally used *The Phoenix Cards.* There are twenty-eight cards, each with an image that represents a specific world culture. You'll be drawn to the images that represent the past lives most relevant to your current life. The cards trigger memory and help you uncover the possible sources of current instincts, attractions, and repulsions. They can be used repeatedly for contemplation or meditation, because the influence of various incarnations shifts as you and your life circumstances change.

SELF-HYPNOSIS/MEDITATION

Another way to explore past-life memories is through a combination of self-hypnosis and meditation. I used this method to clarify some past-life clues about Ireland that didn't match up with details I'd already verified. During a past-life regression, I recalled a girl's plan to avoid marriage to a wealthy, older man by becoming a nun. Duty demanded that Nuala marry two men, but eventually she did become a nun.

I found a match for the landscape in my regression in Killarney, but I couldn't find any record of Nuala or her immediate relatives in that area. Granted, much of history goes unrecorded, but I didn't feel that Nuala had been to Killarney.

Why then had I paired that landscape with her memories in my regression? I needed answers, so I asked Dan to question me while I was in a meditative state. These were my impressions: I lived in Killarney during a lifetime different from Nuala's, on a farm and as the female servant of a wealthy master whose name started with the "Mac" (or "Mc") sound. I wore simple, brown leather shoes with a slight point at the toes. Our family had many mouths to feed, so my parents encouraged me to sleep with the master to earn favors. I felt trapped between what I was expected to do and what I knew was right.

After the meditation, I put two and two together. As Nuala and as the servant girl, I was forced to be with an older man for the sake of my family. It didn't matter whether I was rich or poor; the conflict and the expectation were the same in both lifetimes. Since linear time is an illusion, my memories of the two lives bled into one another during the regression.

Thanks to that meditation, I gained a better understanding of those lives and a greater appreciation for my current one. You, too, can use a combination of self-hypnosis and meditation to learn or clarify past-life details.

You can memorize the beginning procedure (grounding/cleansing and hypnotic countdown) and meditations for this method or record yourself reading them. If you choose the latter option, make sure to include moments of silence whenever appropriate. You might also have a friend or spouse read everything to you. If you do work with a partner, he or she should write down whatever you say during the session.

Begin by performing the grounding and cleansing exercise described at the beginning of this chapter. Then sit or lie down in a comfortable position, close your eyes, and breathe deeply. Consciously relax your body, beginning with your feet and ending with your head. Now, visualize the number 5. Take another deep breath, and as you exhale, replace the 5 with the number 4. Breathe in again, and as you exhale, replace the 4 with 3. Continue this process all the way to 1, which you will replace with the following words in all capital letters: PAST-LIFE INFORMATION. By conjuring a mental picture of these words in your mind, you are setting your intention for the meditation. Once more, inhale deeply and exhale. If the image of the words persists, let it fade away. Begin one of the following meditations.

Art Gallery Meditation

Imagine yourself standing atop a high hill that's covered with soft, green grass. It's a comfortable spring day, and a gentle breeze sweeps the grass and cools your skin. You stroll down the hill, and with each step, you become more relaxed. Down, down you go, more and more relaxed until you reach the bottom of the hill. You turn to your left, and there, on the ground before you, is a brick path that leads to a great domed rotunda. Intrigued, you follow the path. It leads to the building's entrance: a tall, white door. You open the door and step inside to find a private art gallery.

As the door closes gently behind you, you cross the wooden floor to the wall directly in front of you. Purple velvet curtains conceal two large paintings hanging side by side. A golden cord hangs beside each curtain, and in a moment, you will pull those cords to open the curtains and display the underlying images.

You approach the purple curtain on the left and pull its cord. The curtain opens, revealing the portrait of a single individual. Is it a male or a female? Do you feel that you were this person, or was it someone you knew in another life? Note the expression, age, and clothing of the individual. Is he/she holding anything? Do the props or the background seem significant?

A brass plaque beneath the frame gives you three important facts. First, you read the individual's name. Next, you read the location where the portrait was painted. Finally, you read the year it was completed.

When you're ready, move to the painting on the right and pull its golden cord. The purple curtain opens to reveal a scene from the same life as the portrait. It's a moment in time, captured on canvas. What's happening? Who's involved? Study the details. You stare at the scene, and suddenly, it springs to life. The action, sound, and other sensations of the moment unfold as they should. Learn what you can. When you've seen what you needed to see, the action freezes, and the scene reverts to a mere painting. You close your eyes and hear a word or phrase that describes something that lifetime taught or gave you.

Turn around, open your eyes, and exit the building. Follow the brick path to its end and step onto the grass. Turn right and climb the grassy hill. With each step, you feel more alert. When you reach the top, count slowly from 1 to 5.

Open your eyes and record your findings.

Mirror Meditation

Imagine yourself standing inside the highest chamber of a tall, round tower. Bookshelves packed with volumes of information line the stone walls. One book in particular stands out from the crowd. It seems to shine with an aura of insight and importance. You cross the chamber, lift the book from the shelf, and place it on a small wooden table in the center of the room. You know in your bones that this volume contains information from one of your other lives and that when you open it, the first page will reveal the place where you once lived and a date that was pivotal to that life.

Open the book and see what's printed inside. Where did you live? When did you live?

The where and the when are valuable clues, and you know how to learn more. You leave the book open on the table and move toward the stairwell. Surefooted, you start down the stone steps. Down, down they spiral, leading you lower and lower, to the tower's ground level. This chamber is empty except for one item, which dominates the wall. A gilded, floor-length mirror hangs before you. Curious yet calm, you advance toward it, then stop about a foot away.

You gaze at your reflection. Before long, a white mist forms within the mirror. It softens the details of your face, then hides them altogether. You see nothing in the glass but white, swirling mist, but it doesn't alarm you. You're certain that the mist will clear, and when it does, you'll see your face again. But this time it will be different; you'll appear as you did in the life indicated by the book upstairs. Slowly, the mist disperses, and you regard yourself as you once were.

Are you male or female? How are you dressed? Do you know your name? Your age? Your birthdate? How do you feel (physically and emotionally)?

Above and behind your right shoulder, another face materializes. You're not surprised; it belongs to someone who was important to you in that life. Can you sense a name? What relationship did you share? Look beyond the façade. Is that person someone you know in your current life? If so, can you sense why you've come together again?

Above and behind your left shoulder, yet another face appears. Again, it feels right that this person should be there. Who is it? How did you know each other? Did he/she follow you into your current life? If so, can you intuit why?

The two faces behind you fade away, and you're left with a decision. Will you conclude your investigation and head back upstairs? Or will you leave the tower and explore this life further?

If you've learned enough for one day, go back up the stairs to the top of the tower. Once there, approach the table and the book that still lies open upon it. Close the book and count slowly from 1 to 5. Then open your eyes and record what you discovered.

If this other life still intrigues you, step back from the gilded mirror. Turn to your left and observe the solid oak door on the wall in front of you. Beyond that door is the life in question; when you exit the tower, you will enter that life. You will see, hear, and experience whatever your soul deems important. Approach the door, open it, and step through into your other lifetime.

Embrace the sights, sounds, and smells that greet you. Note the weather and the approximate time of day. Are you alone or surrounded by others? Go with the experience and do whatever feels natural to you. You can stay in this environment for as long or as short a period as you want. When you're ready, return to the tower, open the door, and step back inside the familiar stone walls. Climb the spiral staircase to the topmost chamber.

On the table lies the book that gave you your first clues about the life you just recalled. It's still open, and if you have further questions, the book can answer them. Simply ask a question and turn the page to see what is written on the next one. Ask another question, and then turn to find the answer on the following page. Continue in this way until your curiosity is satisfied. Then close the book and count slowly from 1 to 5.

Open your eyes and write down all data and every detail you remember from your experience.

Whether you scry, dowse, use cards, meditate, or all of the above, you'll open up a whole new world of experience and information. Actually, that world isn't new; your soul is quite familiar with it right now. You'll simply tap into it.

13

Piecing It All Together

Experience is a great teacher. Although I've given many examples in previous chapters, I'd like to use this chapter to demonstrate how past-life clues weave in and out of everyday life—and into each other—and add up to something bigger. First, let's consider two of my monastic lives: those of Aethelthryth and Hygeburg. Along the way, I'll remind you of key points and strategies you can use to piece together your past lives.

In my case, I'd had several experiences that suggested at least one past life as a nun. So I started by writing down those events, consulting old letters, journals, etc. when necessary. Remember to record your own experiences—past and present—because you never know which detail might lead to a breakthrough.

First, I looked to my childhood. My own memories were important, but I also picked my mother's brain for anything she could remember.

She vividly recalled making a comment about me as our family left Catholic mass one Sunday. "Oh Lord," she sighed. "She's going to be a nun."

Her greatest joy in life was being a wife and mother, and even though I was only seven years old, she hoped I'd find similar fulfillment. So my conduct in church, my rapport with the nuns, and the bliss with which I said my prayers triggered a touch of concern.

Her memory helped me recall my own thoughts and feelings at the time. Whenever I knelt to pray as a child, a cloak of peace and awe wrapped around me, and I felt elevated to another level. Sometimes I spoke to God; sometimes I listened. Always, there was the sense that I could attune myself to "heaven," that the divine lived as much within me as without. And I knew, as I looked from pulpit to pew, every person in that church was cherished, guarded, and surrounded by a host of benevolent spirits.

As parishioners passed me on their way to Communion, I seemed to intuit their feelings. If someone was sad or frustrated, I sent them a silent blessing before turning my attention to the next passerby. Occasionally, a person's emotion was so intense that it flooded through me, and I couldn't focus on anything else until I'd said a prayer for the individual, which seemed to diffuse what I'd absorbed. The instinct to help and to heal within the hallowed walls of a church seemed as natural as breathing.

After considering my childhood, I moved on to my experiences as an adult. Some of them I've already shared. The following were just as important.

When I studied in Sweden at Forsa Folkhögskola, I felt an instant connection with a Russian student I met there. That connection became clearer one winter day, when we traveled together to Vadstena and stayed overnight in the city's fourteenth-century convent. As we strolled around the cloister, the atmosphere struck a chord of conviction within me. Once, in the distant past, she and I had been nuns. I didn't know where we'd lived that life, but for the moment, the location seemed less relevant than the vocation. On that medieval site, enveloped by the past, I was certain we'd come together to make that connection.

The history rested safely beneath conscious memory, just out of reach. Had it been a happy one? If so, it certainly helped to explain my affinity for the Catholic nuns as a child.

Oftentimes, being with the right person in the right place can jog past-life memory. Think back to any kindred-spirit friendships you've made through the years. Did you ever get an odd impression about the two of you during a specific activity or when you went somewhere special?

My friend and I were back in Forsa when I turned twenty-five on April 30. That date is known as *Valborgsafton* in Sweden (*Walpurgisnacht* in Germany), so it was then that I learned the connection between my birthday and the eighth-century nun Walburga. At that point, all I knew was that she was a Saxon nun who'd traveled from Devonshire to Germany, but the information seemed linked with my Russian friend.

A little over a month later, I traveled to England, where I seemed attracted to every historic ruin and stone monument in Devon and Cornwall. My first day in the coastal village of Boscastle, I wandered up the hillside and along a coastal path. The sea breeze was crisp and invigorating, and it had its way with my loose hair as I rested on a high, jagged cliff. I stared down at the undulating, sapphire water and stilled.

You've been here before!

I snapped back to conscious thought. I looked around, certain someone had approached me.

No one was visible. Dazed, I shook my head. The voice had been loud and clear and sounded feminine. I perceived no ill will, only an intention to serve. At the time, I wondered if she was one of my spirit guides. Today, I wonder if my past-life self—the one who lived in that area of England—gave me a valuable reminder.

Remember, spirit guides can give you messages through the psychic sense of clairaudience. So can your soul.

You might've noticed—just as I did once I wrote down these experiences—the synchronicity at play during my time in Sweden and England. Within a short period of time, I bonded with a woman I'd known as a nun, visited a convent with her, learned of the connection between my birthdate and Walburga, traveled to Devon, and received a clairaudient, GPS-like message that informed me of my past-life where-abouts. All six of these events were directly connected to my life as the eighth-century nun Hygeburg.

Thirteen years later, I still didn't know about Hygeburg, but once I wrote down all of my experiences, I felt compelled to call my best friend from Wisconsin, Bożena. She was the one friend with whom I'd shared those English adventures when I returned to the States. Now I told her about the intriguing link between my birthdate and Walburga.

Then she described a recent dream in which she and I were together somewhere near water. It was a peaceful setting, but I seemed to be waiting for something. Dan's father—whom she'd never met in the "real" world—arrived and spoke what she sensed was Irish.

Ooh ... old world, she thought. Then he disappeared.

A bell tolled, and I turned to her in the dream. "Remember 11:00," I said.

It was the last thing she heard before waking. We attempted to interpret the dream, but a full understanding of its significance would have to wait three more years. By then, I had finally cracked the case by researching Hygeburg's life and acknowledging the sense of soul recognition I felt while reading her words.

Pay close attention to your own feelings—i.e., what your soul is trying to tell you—while doing your research. They could help you recognize one of your previous identities. You might also consider the possibility that one or more of your past-life selves shared/shares your personal form of creative expression. Hygeburg's and mine was/is the same.

When my research revealed Hygeburg's connection to the monastery at Heidenheim, I recalled choosing Heidelberg University as my target for overseas study with the Fulbright scholarship. The name simply sounded right, and I was so upset when I didn't win the scholarship to study there. But Heidelberg wasn't where I needed to go to make the past-life connection. Hygeburg had traveled to Germany to live a monastic life under Walburga's guidance. In this lifetime, Walburga wasn't in Germany; she was in Wisconsin, and her name was Bożena!

I sprinted upstairs to the phone and dialed Bożena's number. I was brimming with questions.

"Have you ever felt a connection to convents or monasteries?" I asked.

"Oh yes," she said, "especially the really old ones."

"Have you been to Germany?" I continued.

"Yes. I feel really comfortable there. I've been to Berlin and Dusseldorf, but I've always wanted to go to Bavaria."

Then she recounted her reaction the first time I mentioned Walburga to her. "I got goose bumps! I went online and spent half the day reading about her. I felt strongly drawn to her."

I told her what I suspected. Her intuition told her she had indeed been Walburga in another life.

Suddenly, I remembered her dream about us standing near water, hearing a bell toll. I'd recorded it in a Word document, and something told me to look it up now. I hastened to the computer and read the description to her, ending with my cryptic remark: "Remember 11:00."

"I think this dream is related to your life as Walburga," I said, closing the document, "but I wonder why I mentioned the time."

Then I glanced at the clock. "Oh my God!" I exclaimed. "Bożena, it's 11:00! Right now, it's 11:00!"

It was more than coincidence; it was a confirmation.

In chapter 6, we examined how dreams play a role in past-life recall. Keep in mind that someone else's dreams can be just as important!

At bedtime that night, I leaned over Geoffrey's bed and kissed him. He pushed my hair back from my face and smiled. Then, in a sing-song voice, he said, "Walburga-burga-burga-burga. Walburga-burga-burga-burga."

I stared at him. "What did you say?"

"Nothing," he replied.

When I phoned Bożena earlier in the day, he and Connor were running around downstairs playing "Star Wars" at a volume that should've shattered glass. There was no way he'd overhead my conversation. Was he reading my thoughts?

"Walburga-burga-burga-burga," he said again.

"Why are you saying that, honey?" I asked.

"I don't know," he said. Then he rolled over and went to sleep.

Remember our discussion about children's observations? They say the darnedest things! In this case, Geoffrey seemed to be picking up on Bożena's past-life discovery, my past-life relationship with her, or possibly his own past-life association with us both.

He's never met Bożena in person, but the one time he heard me talking to her on the phone, he interrupted me and asked to speak with her. It's the only time he's done that with someone who isn't family, and the first thing he said to her was, "I love you." The sincerity in his voice was definitely food for thought.

It felt right and good to recognize Hygeburg as one of my past-life identities, but my gut told me I was an Anglo-Saxon nun in another life as well. When delving into your past lives, please remember this example from mine. You might find that you had the same profession in two or more lives or the same theme running through several. Your inner voice will inform you.

In my case, many clues hinted at a monastic life, but it was intuition that told me about the other life as an Anglo-Saxon nun. If I hadn't paid attention to that gut feeling, the data (names, dates, etc.) I researched would've been beyond confusing.

But who was I? Where and when did I live? I sought answers by praying for guidance right before bed. If traditional prayer isn't your thing, you can ask your angels or spirit guides for help in figuring things out. You can also set a firm intention in your own mind that you will dream something that clarifies a specific past life or leads you to other lives affecting you now.

When your dreams give you information, write it down and act upon it—further research, meditation, comparing notes with someone else who's involved, etc.—as soon as possible. The answers you seek might take a few nights to appear in your dreams, so be patient and continue to ask for spiritual guidance and/or set your intention before bed. You might even find that instead of dreams, you'll just wake one morning with a sense of clarity you didn't have before.

My guidance arrived that night in the form of a dream that might well have been astral travel, and I believe Archangel Raziel was responsible. I was standing—perhaps floating, for my feet didn't seem to touch ground—in a cathedral, staring up at a number of stained glass windows. I sensed someone to my left, so I turned. A tall, robed figure (Raziel's classic appearance) regarded me, but I couldn't see his face beneath the hood. He lifted his left arm out and to the side and pointed to my right, which I understood to be east. The image of a long-ship flashed before me but was quickly replaced by what looked like a huge excavation site.

There they dig, he said telepathically. *You are connected. Sutton Hoo.*

Sutton who? I wondered.

He lowered his arm. *Another one,* he continued. *Salisbury. You were there.*

I woke with a start and headed straight for the computer. A number of websites mentioned Sutton Hoo. It was one of the most important Anglo-Saxon excavations in the twentieth century and believed to be the grave of a seventh-century king. His identity was a mystery, but his wealth—buried in a ninety-foot wooden ship—was incredible. Sutton Hoo is located in East Anglia. Since it and the cathedral in my dream seemed connected, I searched the Internet for photos of East Anglian cathedrals and trusted I'd recognize one.

I found a match in Ely Cathedral, known as "the ship of the Fens." I'd never been there (awake, at any rate!), but its octagonal tower was unmistakable. When I read that the cathedral's construction began in 1083, I frowned. The place was right, but the time seemed wrong. I needed to go further back in history.

Intuition—or a helpful spirit—struck again, reminding me of a book on Anglo-Saxon history that had come into my possession seven years earlier. A warrior's mask on the cover gave me chills and acted like a homing beacon. I didn't open the book but knew I had to have it. Even after it was mine, I didn't open it. Lonely and neglected, it waited on the bookshelf.

Until today. I flipped through the pages and discovered that the mask on the cover was one of the great finds at Sutton Hoo.

Interesting, I thought, but I kept going to see if any of the pictures sparked a feeling of recognition.

At long last, I spied a photo that tugged at my memory. It showed the front cover of a book, and the design was so familiar, I knew I'd seen it before. The caption revealed that it was the Gospel book originally buried with the seventh-century St. Cuthbert. Where had I seen it? Was the pattern reproduced on other books? Had I known the man? Was it possible I witnessed his burial?

I remembered my initial fascination with the name of an *Anne of Green Gables* character: Marilla Cuthbert. Her surname intrigued me. In England, Walburga and other girls—and likely Hygeburg—were educated at the Convent of St. Cuthberga, which became Wimborne Minster in the diocese of Salisbury. Was that why I heard the word "Salisbury" in my dream?

Now here was a man named Cuthbert. I found a reference to his arrival at Coldingham Priory on the Scottish border, a decade before an English woman named Aethelthryth (Æðelþryð/Etheldred), who later became a saint, took the veil there.

As I said before, the first time I saw her name, I felt an intense connection to it. But who was she? Did her life experience relate in any way to mine? Time for more research!

Aethelthryth was one of four daughters of King Anna of East Anglia, which happened to be the location of both Ely Cathedral and Sutton Hoo. The father's name rang a bell, and not just because he was a candidate for the unknown king buried at Sutton Hoo. Every time I heard or read the title of the movie *Anna and the King*, I felt the inexplicable urge to move the word "king" in front of "Anna." As far as I knew, Anna was strictly a girl's name, so the impulse had always seemed ridiculous... until now.

I continued reading. When Aethelthryth first married Ecgfrith, she convinced him to respect her vow of perpetual virginity. During that time, she visited her friend (or relative) St. Hilda, abbess of Streonshalh, the monastery at Whitby in Yorkshire.

In my third novel, the Anglo-Saxon heroine's confidante was a woman named Tilda (short for Mathilda), I thought. *Whitby... Yorkshire.*

The first time I read the novel *Dracula*, I honed in on the mention of Whitby and had to find its location on a map. And Yorkshire was where I met up with the Englishman Tom, who had once been Ecgfrith.

What about St. Cuthbert and the Gospel book I recognized? While Aethelthryth lived in Northumbria, she invited many monks and nuns to her home, and he was one of them. She embroidered a stole and maniple for him and gave him many gifts from her own property. Was the book one of them?

Toward the end of her life, she developed a "swelling" under her jaw, thought to be swollen glands or a tumor, which had to be lanced. The same happened to me when I was a baby. Our family doctor had to cut it open and drain the abscess. Gross, I know, but yet another connection.

As you see, research can spark memories from your present life that help you connect to a past one. It doesn't matter whether you're researching a specific person, a place, or a time period. If you remain open to possibility and give your intuition free rein, valuable clues will appear.

Even though I felt strongly connected to both Hygeburg and Aethelthryth, I still needed confirmation. You might feel the same way, and if you're open to psychics, mediums, and channelers, they can definitely help.

I consulted a local channeler who gave me an earful. In one life, I was Hygeburg, and Bożena was Walburga. My best friend from Sweden—with whom I traveled to Vadstena Kloster—had been a nun with me during that life and a previous one, when I was Aethelthryth. In that life, my second husband, Ecgfrith, was the Englishman, Tom; my father, King Anna, was my Swedish ex-boyfriend, Hans. Sylvia's brother, José, was St. Wilfrid, the seventh-century Bishop of York who was Aethelthryth's friend and advisor. My husband, Dan, was Bede, an English monk at a Northumbrian monastery at Wearmouth and Jarrow.

Born near Newcastle-upon-Tyne, Bede knew Wilfrid and actually interviewed him about Aethelthryth. Although he never met Aethelthryth himself, Bede wrote a hymn to her in his *Ecclesiastical History of the English People* and included her in his *Greater Chronicle*.

Like Bede, Dan is a historian, and he studied at the University of Northumbria in Newcastle-upon-Tyne. He's always been fascinated by monastic life, and after he met me—well before he learned of his possible connection to Bede—he started doing the same form of illumination artwork that was practiced in scriptoriums throughout the British Isles. His personal form of creative expression (art) transformed to reflect the monastic lifestyle that was near and dear to both our souls' journeys.

A swarm of correlations resulted from the channeling session. Hygeburg and Aethelthryth were both Anglo-Saxon Benedictine nuns. That explained why the atmosphere—if not the age—seemed right when I visited the Benedictine monastery Kylemore Abbey in Ireland. Mere hours after I left there, I bought *A Guide to Old English* on impulse in one of Galway's used bookstores. Both Hygeburg and Aethelthryth would've spoken Old English. Without knowing it, I was led straight to two of my previous lives.

It's imperative that you include details—even if they seem meaningless at the time—when writing about your experiences. Buying that book seemed like a whim at the time, but years later, once I learned about Hygeburg and Aethelthryth, the proximity of that purchase to my visit to a Benedictine monastery became important.

Now, about the saint thing… I'm an incredibly flawed individual. My husband loves and supports me for better or worse. Connor tells me I'm the sweetest girl in the world. Geoffrey repeatedly says I'm "like an angel," whatever that means. But that's where it ends. I'm the last person in the world who would ever be connected with sainthood!

But when I think of the thousands of people who've prayed to saints over the centuries, it might explain many of my dreams. My whole life, I've dreamed that I fly to people's sides to aid or comfort them. In addition, since the summer of 1993—when I traveled to Winchester Cathedral, where the tenth-century Bishop Aethelwold used St. Aethelthryth as a role model for his Benedictine reform—I've silently sent healing energy, which enters through the top of my head and travels out from my heart, to countless strangers on the street.

Do those dreams and healing impulses flow from general goodwill? Or could they be intuitive responses to past or present prayers for help? Maybe some of the people I've helped in this life prayed for Aethelthryth's help in a past life. It's strange to think about, yet inspiring.

One thing more about Aethelthryth: it was said she had the gift of prophecy and foretold her own death, which occurred on June 23, 679. That same date—in 1989—marked my first trip to Sweden. It is also the traditional date when Scandinavians celebrate Midsummer's Eve. The Danes call it *Sankt Hans Aften*, and they burn straw witches on bonfires to commemorate the burning of witches in the sixteenth and seventeenth centuries. In Sweden, it's a magical night when a girl can divine her future, particularly the identity of her future husband.

The date of Aethelthryth's death was actually a clue to her future lives and to the man she called "husband" in one of them, because June 23—known as the Eve of St. John and Sankt Hans Aften—was also the date on which the ninth-century Thorgestr (Ota's husband) was drowned. So my ex-boyfriend Hans, as Thorgestr, died on the same date as the daughter of his previous identity, King Anna.

Round and round it goes. Where it stops, no one knows.

I hope this quasi case study has helped you see how I learned about past lives and how you can too. Pay attention to your psychic senses. Investigate your childhood and any paranormal events you can recall. Observe and record the details of your experiences and your dreams. Examine the people, places, and things that attract and repulse you. Consider your relationships with family and friends. Dig into the research with an open mind and heart. Listen to your soul in the stillness of meditation. Ask for help from angels, guides, Universal Intelligence (aka God), and people who are attuned to Spirit. All will provide insight into who you are and who you've been.

DETAILS, DESIGN, AND DESTINY

Discovering just one past life can alter your perspective. Learning about several brings a level of awareness that will change your life. You'll begin to see the magic in the details, the beauty of the design, and the limitless destiny that is not only yours but everyone's. With awareness as our goal, let's step back from the individual lives I've shared with you and consider them from a relational point of view.

Recurring Details

Upon review, it's clear that a single detail can point to a plethora of "past" (i.e., simultaneous) identities. When that one detail—a date, name, place, etc.—is repeated over a number of lifetimes, it's significant. Noting/recording the details you uncover is crucial, because that's how you'll notice the recurring ones and begin to contemplate their meaning.

One example from my life is my favorite holiday, Halloween, which links to several lifetimes working magic in the British Isles and matches the feast day of the mysterious Gwendolyn, Abbess of Wales. Additionally, a number of sources claim that Black Hawk died on October 31 (not October 3). Even All Saints' Day suggests a connection with several people: St. David, St. Gwen, Aethelthryth, and Walburga.

Another example is June 23, the traditional date for Midsummer celebrations and the night when Danes throw straw "witches" onto bonfires. In the Swedish tradition, girls kept watch at springs, hoping to glimpse the reflection of their future husbands in the water. That same date marked the deaths of Aethelthryth—who would be a witch in later lives—and her future self's (Ota's) Norse husband Thorgestr, who was ritually drowned. June 23 also coincides with my first trip to Sweden, a country whose language led me to the boyfriend who'd been not just Thorgestr but King Anna, Aethelthryth's father.

What about the word *beo* in my sons' twinspeak? When paired with Geoffrey's drawing of "the first time we met"—which contained both Vikings and Native Americans—it suggests not only a connection with Leif Eriksson but with Black Hawk as well. Beothuk and Meskwaki-Sauk both belong to the Algonquian language subgroup. It's even been postulated that Algonquin is partly derived from Old Norse.

Take Thursday—my favorite day of the week and the day my twins were born—and its link to the Norse thunder god, Thor. Now consider the following: (1) thunderstorms are believed to increase paranormal activity; (2) St. David was supposedly born during a thunderstorm; (3) Ota's husband was Thorgestr (Old Norse) or, to the Irish, Thorgils, "the servant of Thor"; (4) Thorgunna named her son Thorgils; and (5) Black Hawk was part of the "Thunder Clan."

If I wanted reminders of these connections in my present life, what better birthplace could I have chosen than Florida, the thunderstorm capital of the United States? My lifelong love of thunderstorms can't be coincidence, especially since my father and Irish cousin were both struck by lightning and I, myself, fell five yards short of being thus struck.

On a different note, Aethelthryth the saint and Ota the seer shared an interesting connection. As previously stated, Ota would've known that the wolf was one of Odin's sacred animals. Aethelthryth was a descendant of King Wuffa ("Little Wolf"), after whose reign East Anglian kings were called Wuffings. As part of the Wuffing dynasty, Aethelthryth's ultimate ancestor was believed to be the father-god Woden (Odin). And here's another correlation: Aethelthryth's name is often anglicized to Audrey, and Ota is sometimes referred to as Aud.

Aethelthryth knew St. Cuthbert, and Hygeburg was schooled at the Benedictine nunnery of St. Cuthberga (Wimborne Minster). Aethelthryth's abbey in Ely was just a few miles from the town of Witchford, and Wimborne Minster is only a few miles from Witchampton. The German cloister where Hygeburg lived with Walburga was called *Heidenheimer Kloster,* literally "Heathen-home Cloister." Strange, but true.

The Isle of Man—once a haven for druids—was home to the witchcraft museum founded by the wise man I met in Devon. Man was also the probable base from which the Viking fleet headed by Thorgestr (Ota's husband) invaded Ireland. Centuries later, the Irish Niall Garv O'Donnell (Nuala's husband) died there. My dream about Niall Garv's imprisonment stressed Beaumaris, and nearby Conwy was the area where my guide Gwendolyn was convicted of witchcraft. The castles of Beaumaris and Conwy were part of Edward I's "iron ring" to contain the rebellious Welsh.

Speaking of rings, the English Aethelthryth and the Irish Nuala were both forced to marry twice before becoming nuns. Aethelthryth's East Anglian abbey was in Ely. Nuala's grandfather, Tiege O'Carroll, was the King of Ely.

Ross-Errily, the abbey where Nuala took the veil, isn't far from the monastery of Clonmacnoise, where Ota gave prophecies from the high altar. Ota's husband, Thorgestr, conquered monasteries; Nuala insisted on founding one in Donegal (in Irish, *Dun na nGall*, "fort of the foreigners"). Donegal's monastery compiled the *Annals of the Four Masters*, which made much of my research possible. Interesting, too, that two of my past-life husbands had it out for monasteries: Thorgestr captured them and Henry VIII dissolved them.

The Irish called the Norwegians—which Ota and Thorgestr (as a Vestfold prince) would've been—either *Finngheinnte*, "white" or "fair foreigners," or *Fionnlochlonnaigh*, "white Lochlanns" (men of the lochs). Nuala's full name, Fionnula, means "fair shouldered." Gwen in Welsh means "white." Between Ota, Nuala, and Gwendolyn, there are an awful lot of "whites" and "fairs" floating around! In addition, my mother and a considerable number of friends (many of whom I didn't mention) were nuns and/or worked white magic in previous lives.

Along the way, ravens and wolves have appeared and reappeared, forging links between pagan and Christian traditions. Ravens, in particular, signify two cities where I've lived:

(1) Lyons, during a life in pre-Renaissance France, and (2) London, in this life and Katherine Howard's. Apparently, the site for the town of Lyons was selected when a flock of ravens settled there. Across the Channel, the Tower of London keeps ravens, purportedly because of a legend that predicts the fall of Britain if ever they leave the grounds. The resident ravens have had some inspired names, among them Hugine and Munine (Odin's ravens), Thor, and Bran (the raven-god).

One connection after another! They're not only intriguing, but they help connect the dots. Write down the details of your different lives—names, dates, places, etc.—as you learn about them and see how they relate to each other. Pay close attention to the ones that pop up again and again. Your life story—i.e., your lives' stories, which are your soul's story—is unique. Only you can connect its dots.

Archetypes by Design

I believe that each of us—at one time or another—experiences the full spectrum of the human condition by playing every role imaginable on a greater stage than we can fathom. Yet, as you learn about other lifetimes, you might find that a few prominent archetypes (e.g., the hero, the maiden, the magician, the trickster, etc.) appear repeatedly. Your angels, guardians, and guides—who serve your highest good at all times—can help you see these patterns. They collectively agree on which of your other lives are most meaningful and enlightening for your current lifetime, and they can trigger past-life memories to bring specific symbols and archetypes into your awareness.

In her book *Bringing Your Soul to Light*, Dr. Linda Backman refers to these benevolent beings as one's "spiritual team," comprised of spirit guides and wise elders who coordinate the spirit realm and our interaction with it. She explains: "The client's spiritual team chooses the best messages to convey. They may want to nudge a person to alter something about the present life, or they may simply wish to support the client to maintain and enhance the course of the current incarnation." Either way, the triggered memories will enhance your spiritual growth and help you achieve the destiny your soul chooses.

Let's look at the archetypes that dominate the lives I've uncovered. The **prophet/prophetess** emerged as the Stone Age astrologer and "reader of the bones," the Egyptian astrologer, Aethelthryth, Ota, and Thorgunna. The **wizard/enchantress** and the **healer** guided Thorgunna, Gwendolyn's apprentice, the English "witch," and the Native American healer. The **princess** influenced Aethelthryth and Nuala, and the **queen** held sway over Aethelthryth, Ota, and Katherine. And while the **nun** lived through Aethelthryth, Hygeburg, and Nuala, only Ota accepted the role of **priestess**.

I know those archetypes influenced other lives not included in this book, and since I'm female this time around, it makes sense for me to connect with them during a lifetime when I inhabit that gender. Perhaps I've accessed these specific lives because they address issues I'm currently working on or parts of myself I need to express. The **artist** archetype dwelled in Hygeburg, as it does in me. Both of us felt a responsibility to channel the music and magic of writing into a way to serve Spirit.

Do you recognize the themes running through my life? A search for the sacred. The need to commune with the divine and to be of service.

The lives I've recalled include many different spiritual traditions. My friends in this life also belong to a number of religions/spiritual traditions: Native American, Hindu, Buddhist, Muslim, Jewish, Christian, Wiccan, etc. Even as a child, I experienced several forms of Christianity. It's almost as if I encountered various interpretations of Spirit in order to see the commonalities and move beyond the need to follow one specific path. By acknowledging the value in all paths, my—and everyone's—inseparable connection to the divine became crystal clear. Now, I can serve others by reminding them of that connection, thanks to the artist archetype that compels me to write.

Of course, I can't help but review the roles some of the men in my life have played. Dan was and is a lover, husband, and best friend. As Bede, his fascination with Aethelthryth prompted him to write about her, which enabled me to research that other part of myself. José, twice a foreign ambassador, was a friend, advisor, uncle, and lover. Hans was a father, husband, accuser, and lover, not to mention King of Dublin (Thorgestr) and King of East Anglia (Anna). It's worth noting that he returned to East Anglia in a later life as a self-proclaimed Witchfinder General. Did his delusions of grandeur and need for control result from his previous lives as king?

As Thorgestr, he was drowned; as Matthew Hopkins, he drowned others. But while he was still in his twenties, Hopkins died of tuberculosis. According to Essex legend, his ghost haunts Mistley Pond, especially around the dates of witches' sabbats. Does a part of Hans wander that part of England even now?

Interwoven Destinies

As we've seen, one detail, place, or moment in time can touch a number of lifetimes. When that happens, you experience what I like to call a mystical intersection. It feels like destiny because it is destiny; you chose that detail, that place, that moment, before birth to remind yourself of your immortal Spirit. You're at the right place at the right time—sometimes with the right people—for several threads to come together.

One example is my twenty-fifth birthday, when I learned about the various traditions associated with my birthdate. I already knew it was important to the Celtic calendar and a witches' sabbat, but then I discovered its association with the Anglo-Saxon Walburga, a nun I actually knew when I was Hygeburg. I also learned the Norse tradition, which honored Odin's symbolic death—when he hung upside down on the World Tree for nine days in an act of self-sacrifice—and his rebirth with the knowledge of runes, to be used for magic and writing. On the night of April 30, the wall between the living and the dead supposedly crumbled. To me, that date was starting to represent a point at which the veil separating my many lives thinned. I had to smile when a Swedish friend explained it all.

A Saxon nun who traveled from Devonshire to Germany. Celtic custom and Norse mythology. Witchcraft and writing.

"My birthdate couldn't be more perfect if I planned it," I told her.

An inner voice whispered, *You did.*

Another example is when my Irish cousins took me to visit Clonegal Castle (aka Huntington Castle) during my first trip to Ireland. It was their idea to show me a "witches' castle," even though they knew nothing about my past-life connection to witchcraft. How could they? I didn't even know about it yet!

Their easy acceptance of pagan customs alongside Christian convention was refreshing, and I reveled in our outing. The castle was both an ancestral home and the Foundation Centre of the Fellowship of Isis. Its gardens were said to be the second oldest in all of Ireland, and there was even a grapevine brought as a cutting from a vine planted for Anne Boleyn at Hampton Court Palace. The Avenue of Yew Trees was supposedly planted by Franciscan monks more than 600 years earlier, and I learned that the yew was one of the nine sacred trees used for kindling the fires of Beltane. At the time, I couldn't escape the impression that I was meant to be there, that ancient traditions of white magic—be they Celtic or other—were essential to my makeup.

Little did I know, that one visit to Clonegal Castle held clues to several lifetimes. As the home of the Fellowship of Isis, it related to a life in ancient Egypt that included Dan, our sons, the teacher I recognized as Anne Boleyn, and her two daughters. The castle's prized grapevine reflected my life as Katherine Howard and the tragic events that occurred at Hampton Court Palace. The Avenue of Yew Trees, planted by Franciscans, connected to my life as Nuala, the Irish, Franciscan nun, and during my third trip to Ireland, when I explored the fifteenth-century ruins of Muckross Abbey, a large yew tree as old as the abbey itself was my only companion. It was there inside the abbey that I realized I'd been a nun in the 1400s and glimpsed a monk's ghost in a timeworn stairwell. (Was the apparition evidence of a residual haunting, or could I have picked up on the tree's memories?) Because the yew is sacred to the Beltane fires, the yew walk at Clonegal Castle led to everything linked with April 30. During those few hours at the "witches' castle," I was smack-dab in a mystical intersection.

You are constantly creating. Your choices in every lifetime weave your destiny. So do mine. All of our destinies weave together to create humanity's destiny and—when combined with the destinies of every sentient being in the universe—the realization of God's desire to know himself/herself/itself experientially.

Our souls—which are part of God/Universal Intelligence—desire it, too. They give a portion of themselves to each incarnation we experience so that in the final analysis—and in moments of meditative silence or joyful reunion—we feel the bliss of who we really are: one spirit. Limitless. Universal. Whole.

Our past, present, and future lives are interwoven realities, not unlike the distinctive landmark near Black Hawk's cabin. They're like trees with interwoven roots and branches, reaching toward each other, the rest of the forest, and the sky. When we step back, view them, and consider their relationship, we do more than validate our immortality; we experience our souls, and indeed the One Soul. We become, even if just for a moment, the "unobserved observer," the one who sees it all and knows all of it as perfect.

14

LASTING BENEFITS

Now for the lasting benefits you'll gain from past-life discovery! They are spiritual evolution, remembrance, and transcendence. Let's consider all three.

SPIRITUAL EVOLUTION

All souls were created at once and exist in "the eternal now," but in the material world, time and evolution exist. The soul has a natural desire to expand, and our every choice and experience impact it. We are constantly evolving, "maturing" in our ability to know ourselves as one with each other and with God/Universal Intelligence. Seen in a linear light—i.e., time moving in a straight line in one direction—each successive life produces more enlightened personalities.

We live in the third dimension, but that dimension is influenced by the higher ones. Our nearest neighbors are the fourth dimension, aka the astral plane—the energetic vibration immediately beyond the physical plane where ghosts reside and some telepathy, out-of-body experiences, and mystical events occur—and the fifth dimension, aka the Other Side—the higher vibration of the spirit world where our spirit guides and guardians live and where we live between lifetimes. Contrary to popular belief, fourth-dimensional experience isn't weird or spooky; it's a natural extension of our third-dimensional awareness and a bridge to fifth-dimensional wisdom.

Yet our souls are always aware of their timeless nature. They know that the evolutionary journey—like time—is an illusion. In every moment, the soul is exactly who and where it longs to be. And thanks to free will, there's nothing we have to do in this life or any other.

As "God" says in Neale Donald Walsch's *Conversations with God* (Book 3):

You may "come back" as anything you wish, or in any other dimension, reality, solar system, or civilization you choose. Some of those who have reached the place of total union with the Divine have even chosen to "come back" as enlightened masters. And, yes, some were enlightened masters when they left, and then chose to "come back" as *themselves* … There is nowhere to go, nothing to do, and no one you have to "be" except exactly who you're being right now.

The master teachers of the world, such as Babaji, Buddha, and Jesus, knew—and indeed, know—this truth, and they tried to share it with humanity so that we could end the daily struggle. They essentially "collapsed time" and embraced their soul's true identity by knowing themselves as one with their source.

REMEMBRANCE

Many people see life as a school and reincarnation as a tool through which we learn. Yet our souls—our true selves—already know everything there is to know. We have only to remember. As "God" explains in Neale Donald Walsch's *Friendship with God*, teaching isn't about putting knowledge into someone; it's about drawing it out. "The real Master knows he has no greater knowledge than the student, only greater memory."

When we remember parts of our other lives, we are literally "re-membering," bringing different parts or "members" of our soul back into our consciousness, back into the fold. We are becoming whole again, one again.

On the night that thirty-five-year-old Siddhartha Gautama became the Buddha ("awakened one"), he remembered all of his past lives while meditating under a large, sacred fig tree, which was later called the Bodhi ("wisdom") tree. During that meditation, he perceived the true nature of the universe and achieved enlightenment.

The spiritual path is about expanding your awareness, raising your consciousness to know and live a larger reality. Your perception of your identity shifts from an individual perspective to a relational one. Even in one lifetime, you play a number of roles: daughter, sister, wife, mother, etc. Over a series of lifetimes, those experiences are compounded and coalesce into an amazing performance that is nothing short of a miracle. Remembrance is the key that opens the door to that expanded reality.

TRANSCENDENCE

The dictionary defines "transcend" as follows: to go beyond a limit or range; to surpass something in quality or achievement; to exist above and apart from the material world. I would add the following: to experience the vastness of one's soul; to know that one's true self is limitless and universal; to feel one's unity with everything in existence. Think about it: if we're all one spirit, then two people recalling the same lifetime makes perfect sense because in the final analysis, we're all everyone!

Transcendence is freedom. Learning about past lives can light the way. You needn't identify yourself wholly as the person/ego you took on this time around. You are that person, yet you are more. You are in the world, but not of it. You, the microcosm, become the macrocosm, and so transcend it.

Sometimes, at least!

Margaret Wolfe Hungerford wrote, "Beauty is in the eye of the beholder." The soul sees beauty everywhere: splendor, symmetry, connection, value… in any experience. To learn about other lives, you have to get in touch with your soul. You have to see, hear, and feel with your larger self. The more you do so, the easier it will be to view your current life and circumstances as your soul does, as something beautiful.

As you contemplate your soul's journey and evolution, you'll remember more and more of yourself—your many selves—and begin to transcend what many still view as a one-time, finite existence. You'll know that you're part of something bigger and start to feel your connection with everyone and everything. As your awareness expands, you will sense things from your "past" and "future" and feel them blend into an all-encompassing, perfect present. The everyday world will become, in a word, magical.

CONCLUSION

A reputable channeler once told me I was a teacher of the weaving of fate on the Other Side. Gwen ferch Ellis was a weaver; it would make sense if she was my guide in spirit as well as the flesh. It's only fitting that the spider is one of my totems, and it delivered a message more specific than I initially realized.

Spider wasn't just telling me to write. It was telling me what to write: about the weaving of destiny through lifetimes and relationships that are inextricably linked.

Our experiences are like threads, weaving in and out of a number of realities. The themes running through our many lives—warrior, seeker, savior, etc.—strengthen with each repetition, creating variant, vibrant colors in a cosmic tapestry of the soul. I've discovered a mere patch of the patterns designed by and for Spirit, but it's given me a glimpse of the larger tapestry that stretches between all of our lives—and all life—through the infinite mind of God. I'm grateful for the view, and for the opportunity to share it with you.

Explore your past lives, if it feels right to do so. Your angels, guardians, and guides will help you see what matters most to your health, happiness, and spiritual progress. Your awareness will expand, and your soul will celebrate.

Recommended Reading

Andrews, Ted. *How to Uncover Your Past Lives.* Woodbury, MN: Llewellyn Publications, 2006.

Backman, Dr. Linda. *Bringing Your Soul to Light: Healing Through Past Lives and the Time Between.* Woodbury, MN: Llewellyn Publications, 2009.

Bercholz, Samuel, and Sherab Chödzin Kohn, eds. *The Buddha and His Teachings.* Boston, MA: Shambhala Publications, 2002.

Bernstein, Morey. *The Search for Bridey Murphy.* New York: Doubleday, 1989.

Brocas, Jock. *The Everything Guide to Past Life Experience: Explore the Scientific, Spiritual, and Philosophical Evidence of Past Life Experiences.* Avon, MA: Adams Media, 2011.

Browne, Sylvia. *Life on the Other Side: A Psychic's Tour of the Afterlife* (audiobook, CD). Minneapolis, MN: High-Bridge, 2005.

———. *Phenomenon: Everything You Need to Know About the Paranormal*. New York: Dutton, 2005.

———. *Psychic Children: Revealing the Intuitive Gifts and Hidden Abilities of Boys and Girls* (audiobook, CD). Minneapolis, MN: HighBridge, 2007.

Bruce, Robert, and Brian Mercer. *Mastering Astral Projection: 90-Day Guide to Out-of-Body Experience*. Woodbury, MN: Llewellyn Publications, 2004.

Danelek, J. Allan. *The Case for Reincarnation: Unraveling the Mysteries of the Soul.* Woodbury, MN: Llewellyn Publications, 2010.

MacLaine, Shirley. *It's All in the Playing.* New York: Bantam, 1988.

———. *Out on a Limb.* New York: Bantam, 1986.

McClain, Florence Wagner. *A Practical Guide to Past Life Regression.* St. Paul, MN: Llewellyn Publications, 1985.

Merivale, Ann. *Souls United: The Power of Divine Connection.* Woodbury, MN: Llewellyn Publications, 2009.

O'Neill, Kim. *Communicating With Your Angels* (audio CD). Houston, TX: Casablanca Productions.

———. *How to Talk with Your Angels.* New York: Avon, 1995.

Schucman, Helen. *A Course in Miracles.* Mill Valley, CA: Foundation for Inner Peace, 2007.

Tucker, Jim B. *Life Before Life: Children's Memories of Previous Lives.* New York: St. Martin's Griffin, 2008.

Virtue, Doreen. *Healing with the Angels: How the Angels Can Assist You in Every Area of Your Life.* Carlsbad, CA: Hay House, 2004.

Walsch, Neale Donald. *Conversations with God: An Uncommon Dialogue (Book 1).* Charlottesville, VA: Hampton Roads, 1995.

———. *Conversations with God: An Uncommon Dialogue (Book 2).* Charlottesville, VA: Hampton Roads, 1997.

———. *Conversations with God: An Uncommon Dialogue (Book 3).* Charlottesville, VA: Hampton Roads, 1998.

———. *Friendship with God: An Uncommon Dialogue.* New York: Putnam, 1999.

Webster, Richard. *Encyclopedia of Angels.* Woodbury, MN: Llewellyn Publications, 2009.

Weiss, Brian L., M.D. *Many Lives, Many Masters: The True Story of a Prominent Psychiatrist, His Young Patient, and the Past-life Therapy That Changed Both Their Lives.* New York: Fireside, 1988.

Wilde, Lyn Webster. *Celtic Inspirations: Essential Meditations and Texts.* London: Duncan Baird Publishers, 2004.

Wiseman, Sara. *Your Psychic Child: How to Raise Intuitive and Spiritually Gifted Kids of All Ages.* Woodbury, MN: Llewellyn Publications, 2010.

To Write to the Author

If you wish to contact the author or would like more information about this book, please write to the author in care of Llewellyn Worldwide Ltd. and we will forward your request. Both the author and publisher appreciate hearing from you and learning of your enjoyment of this book and how it has helped you. Llewellyn Worldwide Ltd. cannot guarantee that every letter written to the author can be answered, but all will be forwarded. Please write to:

Judith Marshall
% Llewellyn Worldwide
2143 Wooddale Drive
Woodbury, MN 55125-2989

Please enclose a self-addressed stamped envelope for reply, or $1.00 to cover costs. If outside the U.S.A., enclose an international postal reply coupon.